Living in America

Hilarious and Provocative Tales
of a Foreign Student

Dr. Eric E. Clarke

Published by the Johnson Tribe Publishing House, LLC
Atlanta, GA

Copyright © 2016 by Dr. Eric E. Clarke

All rights reserved, including the express right to reproduce this book or portions thereof in any form whatsoever whether now known or hereinafter developed.

Johnson Tribe Publishing House
P.O. Box 1587 Powder Springs Georgia 30127
888-400-7302
info@johnsontribepublishing.com
www.JohnsonTribePublishing.com

Manufactured in the United States of America
10 9 8 7 6 5 4 3 2 1

FIRST EDITION – March 2016
Creative Direction: Eric E. Clarke
Book Design: Stacey Bowers, August Pride, LLC

ISBN-10: 0-9896733-8-3
ISBN-13: 978-0-9896733-8-9

USA $12.95
Canada: $15.00

Dedication

To my wife Irma without whose dedication and support my successes in life would not have been possible. To my wife Frances whose encouragement and patience inspired me to write about my experiences during my student years and beyond. I thank my dear friends (brothers) Dr. Augustus (Owen) Godette and Keith Hazlewood for enriching my life.

Contents

Prologue 1

Chapter One: My Motivation to Immigrate to America 4

Chapter Two: My Trip from British Guiana (Guyana) : to College 7

Chapter Three: Getting Acclimated to College Life 12

Chapter Four: Finances 21
    Keeping Up With College Expenses 21
    My First Christmas 23

Chapter Five: Driving in America 25
    Getting My Driver's License 25
    The 1948 Pontiac 27

Chapter 6: Extraordinary Events 29
    Unusual Experiences on Trips from: College to New York City 29
    Scheme to Get Cheap Car Rides to New York 30
    The Diarrhea Incident 31
    My Trip to Louisville, Kentucky 32
    Visiting a Friend in New York City 34
    The Burning Hair 35
    An Embarrassing Moment 35
    The Suckling Pig 36

Chapter Seven: Food 37

Chapter Eight: Racial and Cultural Challenges 41

Chapter Nine: Summers in New York while at College 58

Chapter Ten: Jobs while in College 62

Chapter Eleven: Musical Exploits 67

Chapter Twelve: My First Jobs Following Graduation 73

Chapter Thirteen: Handling Money 77

Chapter Fourteen: Family 79

Chapter Fifteen: Educating Our Children 88

Support Groups 91
Chapter Sixteen: The Impact of Language, Culture and Discipline on the Possibilities for Success 93
Epilogue 96

Prologue

I came from humble but enriched beginnings, attributed to the examples set by my parents and five older siblings, their love, and their support. I remember how my father garnered the respect of colleagues and persons in high positions, even though he only had an elementary education. A dedicated family man, he had great presence. He and Mom ensured we children stepped out in simple clothing but immaculate from head to toe. Dad insisted on well-maintained and shiny shoes; he spent many Sundays resoling and shining or teaching us how to shine shoes. He had learned the shoemaking trade as a teenager, but never pursued it as a vocation. Dad worked for as long as I knew him as the senior messenger of The Royal Bank of Canada. He wore a khaki suit with silver buttons. Mom kept his suits and shirts spotless and well pressed, washing and pressing them by hand; the children kept his buttons and shoes sparkling.

My mother, though a homemaker epitomized industriousness. She laundered Dad's uniforms, reared chickens and turkeys and kept the family well fed. Dad's friends complimented him on the quality of food at our home. Mom made delicious pastries. She made scrumptious meat patties; everyone marveled at the texture of the crust; it seemed to melt in the mouth. She catered many functions for the bank where Dad worked.

Mom cared about the welfare of others. It started with home. When my sisters got married and begun to raise families, Mom would get up at 4:00 a.m. to go and take care of them and their babies, despite Dad's protestations. She bought fresh vegetables and meats at the local market daily for my sisters and our household. She rode a bicycle and would have a bag of groceries on each side of the handle (one for each sister) and a bag on a carrier at the back of the bicycle for our home. The major grocery in the city delivered a large box of staples to our home every Thursday. When it arrived, Mom would prepare ten or more small bags of groceries and have me deliver them to neighbors and friends, less fortunate. Dad complained about the grocery bill and Mom would say, "You think food is cheap!" We (the children) promised to keep Mom's secret, but I would threaten to tell Dad about the groceries when Mom whipped or scolded me; I admired Mom's generosity. As an adult, I expressed to her my admiration. Once a year, Mom brought a dozen or more persons from an Alms-house to our home and fed them.

Every year for the first twelve years of my life, Mom held a birthday party for me. However, prior to the beginning of the party, she took me to one of the poor homes and had me give out small amounts of money to the residents. I still remember each resident as he or she received the few pennies saying, "God bless you." Having completed our mission we returned home for the party.

Mom wore stylish clothes. My eldest sister made her clothes, and her good friend Aunt Maude made her lovely hats and gloves. In fact, Mom and her two living sisters wore gloves on a regular basis, unusual for black women in Guyana who wore gloves as part of a bride's entourage or on special occasions. Mom and her sisters likely adopted their style of dress from the European women who rode in the carriages operated by their father's livery.

I won a partial scholarship to attend high school, but Mom and Dad still sacrificed to pay the remaining tuition. My siblings accomplished a great deal without a high school education. My eldest sister, Edna, an excellent seamstress could duplicate any design from a pattern, picture or seeing it on a person. My second sister, Marjorie, taught herself bookkeeping and managed a spray-painting business. My third sister, Waveney, owned a commercial hog, fruit and vegetable farm. My eldest brother, Benjamin, considered the best auto body mechanic in the country also owned a driver education school. My older brother Samuel went to England, graduated from college, and became a social worker in Essex.

I learned invaluable lessons from older relatives that prepared me for adulthood. One occasion a friend and I fought under a tamarind tree because he picked up the fruit that I knocked out of the tree. Angry, I tried to denigrate his parents. As the words came out of my mouth, I received a thunderous slap on the back of my head. It came from my older cousin, Eileen, who overheard me; she made me apologize. Another occasion, I raised my hand to hit a female playmate when Aunt Ada, a neighbor (not a blood relative) grabbed my arm and told me only a coward boy would hit a girl. A third incident gave me a "self-taught" lesson. My friend Eulene's Mom had given me permission to take her to a matinee. When I went to take Eulene to the show, her Mom told me Eulene went with friends to a picnic. I had an invitation to the same picnic, so I decided to stop by. When I got there, the boys who knew I had a matinee date with Eulene teased me that she stood me up. Their teasing heightened my disappointment that she went to the picnic instead of the matinee with me that I said unpleasant words to her. Embarrassed in front of her friends and tearful, she went home and complained to her father. He came to our home and complained to my Mom who expressed great disappointment in my behavior; she made me apologize to Eulene and her father. Afterward, I felt sad that I had hurt someone because of my misplaced pride. I was eleven years old at the time and pledged never to hurt anyone in that manner in the future. Throughout the years following that incident, I have never responded in anger to anyone's words.

Chapter One

(renamed Guyana after independence in 1966)

My Motivation to Immigrate to America

At the time I left British Guiana (renamed Guyana after independence in 1966) in February 1958, it remained a British colony and followed the British education system, which provided an elementary education but no further. To achieve a high school education, a student had to win a scholarship or possess the means to pay the tuition. When I attended high school, students had three chances to pass the Senior Cambridge examination administered by Cambridge University in London, which gave them the designation as a high school graduate. It provided the only record of a high school education. A limited opportunity existed to go beyond high school in Guyana at the time. Cambridge University offered an "inter-Baccalaureate" degree in certain social sciences such as History, etc., but few students took advantage of the opportunity – I knew of no one. Students without a path to high school turned to vocational training to secure their future. High school graduates either went into the civil service or continued to obtain certification in nursing, pharmacy, land survey, etc. Individuals applying to the civil service or one of the certification programs had to be eighteen years old.

The lack of opportunity to complete a degree program in British Guiana in 1958 trapped many brilliant students in civil service jobs that deterred them from maximizing their academic potential. Some high school graduates worked in the civil service for a while then went abroad to obtain professional degrees. I graduated much younger than eighteen years, which precluded me from entering the civil service. Therefore, my friend Clifford (in similar circumstances) and I played cricket in a local playground daily for a year and a half. I seem contented to go off and play cricket every day, so Dad wanted to know my plans for the future. I reminded him of my interest in the life sciences, which he and other family members perceived because of my experimentation with frogs. Following our conversation, Dad was able to find a place for me in the pharmacy program though I was under age. While studying pharmacy, I looked forward to an opportunity to go abroad to study, but limited resources remained a major hurdle.

My older brother, Samuel, immigrated to England in 1951. He had no idea where he would stay when he got there or what he would do. He decided to leave Guyana because of an embarrassing incident. A family friend had promised to get him, and a school- mate jobs on a luxury liner and they looked forward to seeing the world through their travels. The would-be sailors gave their parents the date and time of their departure. As a result, Mom and the other mother ensured that they had everything they required for their sea-faring adventure. In addition, a "going away" party took place at our home where family and friends brought gifts and extended best wishes The time for their departure passed and the family friend never showed up. Following their embarrassment, my brother was determined to leave the country; his friend relinquished the idea of traveling. I met the family friend months after my brother left for England, and he told me that he had made the promise in jest.

I eliminated England as a place to further my studies, after hearing the hardships my brother encountered. He told of his difficulty obtaining employment and the nights he slept in telephone booths with newspaper lining his clothes to keep him warm. I decided to go to America instead to further my studies based on information from family friends who lived there. They told of plentiful jobs for college students, and I knew that enrollment in a college gave me a stable home. Fifteen years old and a pharmacy student at the Georgetown hospital, I often spoke of my desire to go abroad to study. A fellow Guyanese Owen Godette, who had come to the hospital to receive training in pharmacy to become a dispenser (nurse practitioner) to provide primary care in rural areas, overheard one of my conversations. Afterward, he told me he had begun arrangements to attend college in America. He had a friend Keith Hazelwood at Central State College in Ohio and planned to join him. Owen and I became close friends, and he urged me to join him at college. The idea intrigued me except I needed a sponsor to guarantee financial support for my course of study. I discussed my need for a guarantor with my Dad, and one of his friends used his business to do so. I received my student visa but knew that no financial support would come from anyone, including my parents once I left Guyana. I would be on my own.

Chapter Two
My Trip from British Guiana (Guyana) to College

On a sunlit day January 1958, I left my home in Georgetown Guyana adorned with my English Wilson felt hat shaped in the popular "pork-pie" style. I wore a Bookers custom-made gray suit (wide knees and small bottoms) and felt a sense of purpose. The entourage that accompanied me to the airport included my parents, brother, sisters, nieces, nephews, other relatives, and friends. They came to send me off into an expectant future filled with lots of hope and promise. As I walked to the awaiting Pan American, propeller driven airplane and sat down; I mused to myself, "Boy, you're on your own!"

The plane touched down later that evening in Curacao, a United States port-of-entry. Upon clearing customs, I spent the night at a hotel before continuing my flight the next morning to Idle Wild Airport (now Kennedy) in New York. I settled in my room on the first floor close to the main thoroughfare. Fearing for my safety, I closed all windows in spite of the intense heat in the room. Hot air poured out of the radiators, which had no controls. I slept well assured of my safety, which turned out to be a delusion because I forgot to lock the door.

The hotel had served breakfast before we went to the airport. At breakfast, I received a small box that read "Rice Krispies" and had flakes similar to the corn flakes I remembered from home. The table had a small jug of milk but no bowls. I wanted to ask the waiter for a bowl but remembered that he only spoke Dutch from our encounter the previous evening when I tried to order postcards. The waiter must have seen my perplexed expression because he opened the box with a knife and poured the milk into it. Waxed paper lined the box - a new experience. Back home, our corn flakes came in large boxes, and we poured some in a bowl with milk.

Our flight arrived in New York the following evening, and I expected a friend to meet me at the airport. He never showed up nor responded to my page. I, therefore, decided to find a quiet spot at the airport and await my flight to Ohio 8:30 the following morning. Relaxed on a lounge chair in a corner awaiting my flight, two skycaps (baggage handlers) approached me, introduced themselves, and asked if they could have some of my Mount Gay rum. They had seen the bottle in my bag as I went through customs. I shared the rum with them, and they sat and chatted with me while consuming over half the bottle. During our conversation, I told them that my parents had a very good friend Aunt Olive in Harlem that I would have liked to see, if possible, before my eight thirty flight the next morning. I decided to call Aunt Olive on the nearby public phone as the two men sat sipping rum. I reached Aunt Olive, and she suggested that I go to Harlem to see her; she would make sure that I got back to the airport in time for my flight. Aunt Olive gave me instructions how to get to the 125th Street subway station, where she would meet me. Her instructions, however, were unclear, because of my unfamiliarity with the places and things she described. One of the skycaps realizing my difficulty understanding Aunt Olive's instructions decided to help. He took the instructions and promised to get me to the subway station.

Finding my way became an adventure. The skycaps gave me the instructions written on a piece of paper, put me on a bus and instructed me to get off at the next stop. I should then catch a cab, give the note with instructions to the driver and he would take me to the 125th street subway station. I got off at the next stop as instructed – a major transportation hub with many buses and taxis. I had to take an escalator to get a taxi. Of course, I had never ridden an escalator. Nevertheless, I stepped on the escalator with my two suitcases and a duffel bag. Almost at the bottom, one of the suitcases slipped out of my hand and knocked the man in front of me off the escalator. Struck with terror, I apologized to the man profusely. He accepted my apology, assured me he was fine and that "things happen." We bade each other good night and left.

Outside the station, a man shouted – "taxi?" He grabbed my suitcases and duffel bag and threw them into the trunk of a taxi. I asked, "How much." He said, "What you got." I gave him two dollars. Entering the cab, I saw another man in the driver's seat, to my surprise. He asked, "Where to?" I gave him the note from the skycap. He looked at the note and said, "I can't read this! Where you want to go Lenox or Lexington?" I shrugged my shoulders. The taxi took off and at the next corner, the driver told me to get out and take a bus around the corner. A bus pulled up a few minutes later; I got on and handed the skycap's note to the driver. He looked at it, handed it back to me and told me to catch the next bus. I got off the bus and decided to go back to the airport and await my flight to Ohio a few hours later.

I whistled for an approaching taxi, recalling what I had seen at the movies. That taxi and the next eight with lit medallions passed me by. Panicked, I began to run onto the road waving frantically at each approaching taxi since I could no longer whistle due to the numbness of my frozen face and lips caused by the cold winter air. Finally, the ninth taxi pulled to the curb, and I returned to the airport. After I had lived in the Country for a while, I realized that occupied taxis had lit medallions.

I arrived back at the airport in an hour. Again, I found a seat in a corner and made myself comfortable until my flight to Ohio. As I settled in, a voice called out, "Smallie, what are you doing here? I thought you were home by now." The skycap who wrote the directions to the subway and his partner stood looking down at me. I told them what happened, and they insisted on taking me to Aunt Olive's in Harlem; I had preferred to stay at the airport and await my flight. I gave in, however, and followed them out the terminal struggling with my luggage, as we walked a long way to their car.

We arrived at Aunt Olive's address at about 2:00 am. I rang the doorbell several times, but no one answered. I glanced at the skycaps, and their expression showed bewilderment. Then I heard Aunt Olive's voice, "Who the hell is ringing my bell this hour in the morning?" I called out to her, and she opened the door. After greeting me with a big hug she asked, "Where were you? I just got back from the subway. I told her I got lost and introduced the skycaps. They stayed around long enough to drink the remainder of the bottle of Mount Gay rum. I thanked them for their help as they left. Aunt Olive and I chatted for a while then went to bed knowing that I had a flight to Ohio at 8:00 a.m.

We woke up a couple hours later, and Aunt Olive called a friend in the adjacent apartment and asked him to accompany us to the airport. I thought her friend had a car; instead, we caught the subway changing trains a couple of times. I struggled to keep up with them toting my two suitcases and duffel bag. Time running out Aunt Olive decided to catch a cab, and we arrived at the airport just in time for my flight.

My KLM (Dutch airline) flight arrived at the Dayton airport around mid-day. Thirsty, I decided to get something to drink in the terminal. I approached a vendor with lots of bottled beverages in his case and ordered an aerated drink. The counter clerk looked at me bewildered. "What do you want?" He questioned. I repeated, "An aerated drink!" Still confused, he called out to the man at the back, "There is an African here, and I don't understand what he wants." The man came to the counter and asked, "What do you want?" I pointed to a Pepsi-Cola, and the man exclaimed, "A pop!" In Guyana, we used the term aerated for all carbonated drinks, differentiating them from homemade drinks.

I took a bus from the Dayton airport to Xenia, where I could have taken another bus to the Central State College campus. Anxious to see my friend Owen, I took a taxi instead. As the taxi pulled up on the campus, students hung out on the lawn in front of a dormitory. The taxi stopped, and I asked some students if they knew my friend. They did and directed me to his room in the building behind them. Owen opened the door, and we hugged, happy to see each other. Unsure of the time of my arrival, I surprised him. His roommate, Keith, the Guyanese who invited Owen and me to attend Central State College had not returned from work at the cafeteria.

Keith returned hours later with his Pan Am bag filled with packets of jelly, crackers and a large jar of pears. Keith, tall and wearing glasses, resembled his older brother whom I met prior to leaving Guyana. The three of us stayed up all night, as I brought them up to date with events at home and they gave me pointers about college life.

The next night we sat drinking Weiderman beer around a roaring fire in a potbelly stove in a little tavern located in Xenia, a small town a few miles from campus. Owen and Keith appreciated the relaxation having completed final exams a few days earlier. An American student Nathaniel, a friend of Owen and Keith, drove us to town. He had an unusual car; he had to back it up for one hundred to two hundred yards, before able to go forward. He parked his car in an open area at the back of the campus to go through the maneuver.

I bunked with Owen and Keith for several days without reporting to the college authorities. The administration put out a missing alert for me because I should have arrived several days earlier according to my letter. We received word of the alert, and I reported to the administration allaying everyone's fear that something might have happened to me.

Owen, Keith and I frequented the tavern until time to get ready for the new semester. John, another Guyanese, met me when he returned to campus a week after I arrived. They told me about a good friend Elwood from the Bahamas who went home for his father's funeral. Elwood returned to campus a week later. On the first night of his return, he and Keith had a farting contest. Incredulous as it sounds, it did take place. Keith kneeled on one bed and Elwood on another. They kept farting one after the other for at least ten minutes – a remarkable feat. I had never seen or heard anything like it before or since. In the end, Owen and John declared the contest a draw.

Chapter Three
Getting Acclimated to College Life

As a tradition, students (at Central State College) dressed up for Sunday dinner. Respectful of the tradition, I got dressed up. On my way to meet Owen and Keith at their room on a lower floor of our dormitory, I stepped out of my room decked out in my very broad brim British Wilson felt hat. A student in the hallway shouted out to the other students, "Hey! There is a cat out here with a whole lot a brim on his head!" Doors flung open, and everyone entered the hallway gawking at my hat. My roommate exiting the bathroom looked at me and exclaimed, "Damn rooms! You got an umbrella on your head." In my embarrassment, I countered, "You guys should learn to appreciate a top quality hat. This is British felt!" With that comment, I retreated to my room and discarded the hat in the trash – I never wore it again. Fashion had passed me by with broad brim out and stingy brim in. I had thought my hat in vogue since my dad had brought back a similarly styled hat from America a few years earlier.

With my other clothing dated, such as my big knee and small bottom pants, I moved quickly to update my wardrobe. I traded my services (pressing shirts, cuffing pants, and haircuts) with my roommate for a sports jacket and pants outfit. I obtained a new suit from Nathaniel. He hacked the suit in the dormitory for seventy dollars – the tag indicated one hundred and twenty dollars. Several students approached him to purchase the suit, but I pleaded that I needed a suit badly. He asked for my offer. I told him to hold on, went to my room and came back with a handful of coins – a dollar and fifty cents worth. Nathaniel could not control his laughter, as

I stood stone-faced. I promised he would get the remainder soon, without giving a specific timeframe. To my surprise, he gave me the suit. As I recall, he received about ten dollars from me in fifty-cents and one- dollar increments; however, I pressed many white shirts for him and gave him several haircuts. I took a picture in the suit and sent it to my parents and fiancée Irma in Guyana. I looked successful in my well-tailored suit, although unable to use the washing machine in the dormitory for thirty cents.

Sticker shock set in when I went to purchase books for my classes; those great nights drinking Weiderman beer had come back to haunt me. I had underestimated the cost of books. Pecuniary embarrassed, one of my chemistry professors allowed me to credit the purchase of the textbook for his class to his bookstore account, as a loan.

I never realized differences exist between British and American - English, weights, and measures - until I began classes. How could a pint have sixteen ounces? I had compounded medicines as a pharmacist in Guyana using twenty ounces to a pint in my calculations for years. Upon investigation, I discovered the origin of the discrepancy. America continued to use the old "Queen Anne" gallon while the Europeans in 1824 changed to the larger "Imperial" gallon. I also had to adapt to major changes in spelling. Words such as favor and parlor no longer contained a "u" and the word "program" lost the "me" at the end. Differences also occurred in the pronunciation of scientific terms as well, including duodenum, capillary and salivary. The word cutlery got quizzical looks from cafeteria staff until someone schooled me to the correct American word, silverware.

Arriving on campus, I had a major deficit in my preparedness that never occurred to me as an essential – I could not type. As a result, I had the most disheartening experience in my academic career. I started college in the second semester and enrolled in a sociology class – a subject alien to me. The class, which began in the first semester, had already covered sixteen chapters. Enrolled in a class in a subject unfamiliar to me and so many chapters behind, I had to study extremely hard to become acquainted with the instructions missed from the first semester and keep up with the current work. I managed the studies but had an unrelated problem. I could not type, had no money to pay for typing, and the professor refused to accept hand-written papers. A female classmate, knowing of my dilemma, offered to type my final paper without charge. I delivered my hand-written paper to her the next morning as arranged. I had to turn it in at 4:00 p.m. the next day. She assured me it will be ready by noon that day, and I should check with her at 10:00 a.m. in case she had questions. I did as requested. We discussed a few issues about the text, and she told me to go to her dormitory at noon to collect the paper. I arrived at the dormitory on time and asked the student at the reception desk to call her room. She came down and told me that the paper will be ready in thirty minutes. Thirty minutes turned into an hour, two, then three hours. Anxious, I asked the student at the reception desk to call her room again. This time instead of coming downstairs, she asked the receptionist to tell me she will be down in twenty minutes. She brought the paper to me in the lobby at 3:30 p.m. I thanked her for her help and headed for the door. I had thirty minutes before the deadline to turn in my paper to the professor. On my way, I decided to check the typed paper. Reading the first few lines, I found six typographical errors. I closed the paper, dejected. I passed the class with the worst grade in my entire academic career.

Starting college in the middle of the school year helped me financially, but made the commencement of college difficult. I missed the usual orientation for new students, and unaware of the need to consult an academic counselor proceeded to select classes on my own. Consequently, I selected classes inappropriate for a freshman. In addition to entering the second semester of a sociology class, I enrolled in a fourth-year psychology course. The professor allowed me to remain in the class, knowing I was new to the subject. She requested, however, that I cut my beard - a symbol of the beat generation and unacceptable to her.

I got a job as a maintenance helper in the science building as part of my student aid program. As a Guyanese trained pharmacist, however, I felt embarrassed for students to see me with a mop and pail. Therefore, as students changed classes I locked myself in one of the bathrooms placing a "Do Not Enter-Cleaning" sign outside until the hallway cleared. Fortunately, my false pride disappeared as I saw other students performing every type of job imaginable throughout the campus. I also discovered the American way - honor in all work. Freed of my pretensions, I swung my mop with pride.

Lack of funds had a deleterious effect on my ability to study due to inadequate sleep. I had little time to sleep working at a restaurant, picking up and distributing mail for the administrative office, mopping floors in the science building and completing my English assignments.

I enrolled in an advanced English class, which required the purchase of two or more magazines each week to complete assignments. Without the means to purchase them, I depended on the generosity of classmates -two Liberian students who roomed together. They allowed me to use their magazines, but I had to wait for them to complete the assignment before I received the magazines to complete mine. I received the magazines at different hours in the morning, sometimes as late as 4:00 a.m. Our class started at 8:00 a.m. Unsure of when I will receive the magazines kept me awake most of the night.

Anxious to fit in with the other students, I decided to adopt their slang. One Sunday on my way to the cafeteria, I met an African student (Phillip); Owen and Keith had recently introduced us. He wore a well-fitted suit, and I told him he looked clean as a yard dog, as a compliment. He did not respond and remained silent as we continued to the cafeteria and had dinner with other students. A couple of days later, Owen asked if I had an altercation with Phillip. He had complained that I insulted him, and he wanted to punch me in the mouth. His complaint puzzled me because my two encounters with Phillip had been cordial. I asked Owen to find out what I had done to offend him. Owen came back and asked if I called Phillip a dog. Phillip had misconstrued my comment as an insult, unfamiliar with the slang. I had heard students greet each other with those words and it never dawned on me that they could have been misinterpreted as an insult based on one's cultural background. I went to see Phillip as soon as I got word from Owen and apologized for inadvertently hurting his feelings.

Robert, another Guyanese student on campus with whom I had studied pharmacy back home exchanged greetings when we met on campus. He seemed interested in my well-being; he would ask,

"How are you doing?" Believing he wanted to know my situation, I gave him a full account of my trials and tribulations. He never shared his challenges. One day he greeted me, "Hello tale of woe." Flabbergasted by his greeting, I felt terrible at first but soon realized that he had done me a favor. I learned an invaluable lesson. "How are you?" is a greeting and not an invitation to unload one's problems, although friends might discuss personal challenges under special circumstances and relationships.

Earl, my first roommate, played the saxophone. He wore fashionable clothes and kept his hair neat with a stocking cap – his doo-rag. He seemed uninterested in academics but practiced his saxophone continually. He and the housemother clashed because he played too loud or late at night. Late one night while Earl played his saxophone, the housemother demanded over the intercom that he stop. He continued and the housemother announced her way to our room. Earl undressed and spread eagle on his bed in the nude. As the housemother entered using her passkey, she gave a loud gasp and slammed the door. Once back in her office, she summoned Earl to come down. Curious, I accompanied him to the office. She admonished him for lying in his bed in the nude; Earl countered that he could be naked in his room if he so chose. The housemother gazed at him, gave a loud sigh and sent him off. The battle between them continued throughout the semester. Earl did not return the next semester, and I wonder if he had a successful musical career. I never received any additional information about him.

Upperclassmen talked a lot about the fun at Friday night dances in the gym. I, therefore, had high expectations for my first experience as a lover of dancing. The gym had a festive atmosphere with students huddled in groups chatting or dancing. I approached a seated female student, bowed, smiled and offered my hand as my British upbringing dictated. An arm reached over my shoulder, grasped her hand and whisked her onto the dance floor. The pattern continued for the next two Friday nights until I adjusted my technique and commanded the dance floor thereafter.

In Guyana, I knew of Jackie Robinson from baseball advertisements at the back of comic books. We never played the game, so I knew nothing about its rules. I had seen games on television in the dormitory, but I paid little attention. I played my first game in a physical education course conducted by Big Jim Walker a former major league football player and coach of the football team. He explained the rules of the game prior to taking the field. My turn at bat I made a hit to mid-field, but instead of discarding the bat and running to first base I headed toward the pitcher with my bat in hand. Threatened by my advance, the pitcher back peddled faster and faster as I approached, shouting, "What did I do?" He thought I would hit him with the bat. The instructor and the other students looked on dumbfounded. After I discarded the bat and apologized to the pitcher, I explained to everyone that I had a mental lapse. I had never played baseball and reacted as though playing cricket where the batters run between the wickets with the bat.

The African and West Indian students formed a soccer team and played against teams from the University of Cincinnati and Ohio State University. I played center forward or right wing. I broke my glasses in a game - an expense I could ill afford, and I decided to play without my glasses thereafter. My first game without my glasses, I moved down the field with little resistance, and I marveled how my game had improved that is until I was about to shoot at the goal. There stood the goalkeeper for my team with an indescribable look on his face. Horrified by my stupidity, I redeemed myself by kicking the ball gently to him. Concentrating on the ball because of my limited vision without my glasses, I had turned around headed toward my own goal as my teammates stepped aside in disbelief. After the game, my teammates demanded that I wear my glasses in future games.

Growing up in Guyana, black athletes ran sprints and long distances equally well. In America, sportscasters and magazines proclaimed that black athletes could not compete with white athletes in long distances because they had a body type more suitable to the sprints. An experience in 1958 while in college debunked that notion.

When the Kenyon Kip Keina won the gold medal in the 1500 meters in Mexico 1968 and the 3000 meters in Munich 1972, he shocked the world. My friends and I knew better. The following account demonstrates why: On a Friday night, a group of us African and West Indian students visited Antioch College eight miles of hilly terrain from Central State College. We went in one car and had to assemble at a particular location for the trip back to campus. One of the African students thought that he had missed his ride back to campus and decided to foot it. The rest of us driving back to campus heard dogs barking. The car's headlights first lit up a pack of dogs and then the shadowy figure of our African college mate running ahead of them. We caught up with him; he had already covered about six miles. When he got in the car, his unlabored breathing for a person who had covered that distance with dogs chasing him surprised us. The fact that he outran the dogs also intrigued us and we asked him to tell us what happened. He explained that initially dogs from one farm ran after him, and as he passed successive farms dogs from those farms joined the chase.

Further, the incident with the African student confirmed my belief that the black athlete's inability to compete in long distance running in America rested with the lack of opportunities for training. Blacks had opportunities to train for the shorter distances because of the many tracks in urban areas. Long distance training, on the other hand, required open spaces and no black man would have thought it prudent to go running long distances in isolated areas in 1958.

I put all my skills to work immediately after my arrival at college. I barbered African and West Indian students in spite the illegality of barbering without a license. I got away with it because I used a razor blade and comb without the sound of electric clippers to give me away. I turned pants cuffs and ironed white shirts as well – many students scorched their white shirts while ironing them. My business started when my roommate asked me to cuff pants and iron a white shirt. Pleased with the results, he boasted about my skills. Soon, other students wanted me to do the same for them.

The American practice of tipping service providers baffled me. I saw it in the movies but never understood the rationale behind the practice. A college mate explained that tips supplement workers' wages. I feel, however, that an adequate wage would better serve workers rather than undependable tipping. Further, a magazine article about tipping incensed me because it asserted that blacks over-tipped because of an inferiority complex. The statement smacked of racism. My first experience with tipping in America occurred while working for the college administrative office. A secretary asked me to buy her a sandwich on my way back from collecting the mail. When I returned, she offered me two quarters as a tip. I politely declined it because I thought the gesture inappropriate for a favor.

In America, expectations when borrowing small sums of money differ from my experience in Guyana. A student asked to borrow a nickel to make a public telephone call. I gave him the nickel without expecting him to return it. He surprised me when he hounded me to repay it. I learned an important lesson about the difference in practice between the two countries. Returning a nickel would have been completely out of my mind, and I would have been embarrassed. In Guyana, I never expected repayment of small sums of money borrowed.

Experiencing winter for the first time, the simultaneous occurrence of sub-freezing cold and sunshine surprised me. I also underestimated the danger of the cold and snow; resulting in frostbite in my great toe. I spent ten days in the infirmary as a result. On another occasion, Owen and I froze on a highway. My first spring, Owen and I hitched hiked from Wilberforce to Columbus Ohio to see one of his friends. When we left campus on the Friday, the weather had been relatively warm for spring, and we received a ride quickly. On our return on Sunday, however, the temperature dropped sharply, and we wore flimsy jackets. Our first ride took us half the way to campus. But, we stood on the highway for a long time without another ride. We decided to find shelter and after walking several miles came to a shopping area. Frozen, we called some friends who lived several miles from where we waited. At first, we sheltered in a store, but it soon closed due to shortened Sunday hours. As a result, we stood in the cold for another hour before our friends came. They lifted us into the car, because of our frozen state. On arrival at their home, they told us that we had to have a cold bath. We exclaimed, "A cold bath!" Owen and I protested. We thought, "We are "frozen" and they want to put us in a cold bath?" Have some mercy! Seeing our anguished expression, our friends explained that the cold water would thaw us out without shocking our system. We reluctantly got in the cold bath and to our surprise, the water felt warm. After the bath, they dressed us in warm robes and gave us hot tea. We stayed at our friends' home for several hours, and they took us back to campus.

I had to adjust to another aspect of college life – the lack of current news from home. Consequently, when a student told me that the Jet magazine had an article about Guyana, I longed to read it and rushed to the library to seek it out. To my consternation, the article pertained to an "Anti-Man Wedding" –the term used in Guyana for homosexuality. I had expected the article to address a subject, which dealt with a more significant aspect of Guyanese life.

I became aware of homosexuality prior to leaving Guyana when the chief pharmacist where I worked teased a clerk that his boyfriend left him and went to England. To satisfy my curiosity, I befriended the clerk. I rode with him on my way home a couple afternoons and pumped him for information. Although reluctant at first, he confirmed the chief pharmacist's accusation. His acknowledgment of his involvement in the activity made me aware that such behavior existed. I stopped riding with him on my way home to his chagrin, in order to disassociate myself from any vestiges of the behavior.

Chapter Four
Finances

Keeping Up With College Expenses

I experienced a lack of adequate funds throughout my college years. As a foreign student, however, I had to overcome my financial difficulties to complete my studies. Unlike American students who could quit school, get a job and continue with their lives, I had one option – return to Guyana in defeat. The thought, unacceptable to me, gave me the impetus to press on. I thought how fortunate for the veterans who attended college supported by the GI Bill, even though many of them squandered the opportunity. They drove around the campus in sports cars paying little attention to their studies. From my observation, female students who befriended the men benefitted from the funds the GI Bill provided. They graduated while their boyfriends languished on campus years after they should have graduated. Some of the male GI Bill students had been in college two years prior to my arrival. I graduated leaving them on campus.

Lodging accounted for a major portion of tuition. Therefore, in my second semester when the opportunity to live in a dormitory slated for demolition at a reduced rate of seventy-five percent, Owen, Keith, I and four other students jumped at it. Each of us had a room with double bunk beds, which encouraged students, including John, without lodging to sneak in and sleep on the extra bed. The hallways and other common areas had heat; the rooms, however, had little or no heat. We, therefore, studied in the recreation room and filled our trash pails with hot water before getting into bed at night. The administration got word of the freeloading students and raided the dormitory at two or three in the morning. Students had to escape through the windows. Later in the semester, the administration condemned the building and moved us to other dormitories.

John, unable to bunk with Owen, Keith or me after the college condemned the dormitory, sought other accommodations. Two white unmarried sisters, sociology professors, allowed him to sleep in their attic accessible from the fire escape. His accommodations had no toilet. At night, he used two sixteen ounce soda bottles as a urinal. John's resolve to complete his final semester commanded my admiration. He succeeded without adequate accommodations or a meal ticket. Throughout that semester, he wore double socks, double sweaters, and a coat because his attic accommodations had sparse heat. He always seemed cold. He jogged continuously when we met outdoors.

My Dad's moral support inspired me to press forward with my ambitions. So, when Owen and Keith suggested that early morning in 1959 on our drive home to Brooklyn NY for the Christmas holidays that my Dad had to die for me to claim manhood, I countered, I would continue as a boy if it meant that he would be alive. We had no idea my Dad lay dying at the very moment of our conversation.

I arrived home in Brooklyn, NY later that morning and went to bed exhausted from late nights studying for examinations and the car trip. I awakened several hours later and checked the mail. It included a cablegram, which I thought came from a family friend who sent out Christmas greetings that way. Instead, it came from Mom in Guyana. It read, "Dad died 4:00 o'clock this morning don't travel, mother." I knew people die suddenly, but Mom's letter two weeks earlier made no mention of illness in the family. Receiving Mom's cablegram about Dad's death made me recall how I agonized over leaving Guyana when he had a heart attack in August 1957, six months before my scheduled departure. As the youngest male child, I wanted to ensure that Mom had adequate financial support in the event that Dad became incapacitated. I had told her I wanted to postpone leaving Guyana because of my concern for her financial well-being. She dismissed my talk of postponing my academic pursuits and demanded that I stick to my plans.

I impatiently waited to tell my finance Irma the sad news. (Irma and I engaged before I left Guyana in 1958 and she had a very close relationship with my parents. She arrived in America in June 1959 to take up a nursing position at a hospital in New Jersey. She lived in Brooklyn where I stayed when away from college). I met her on the subway as she returned from work. When I told her of the cablegram from Mom, she accepted the news much calmer than I expected. Unknown to me, she had received a letter from Mom that informed her of Dad's hospitalization. She never told me about his illness to spare me from worry during my final exams.

I missed hearing my Dad's voice and his encouraging words. However, his death had a beneficial aspect to it. I used his death to help my financial situation at college. I told the college administrative office that my dad died, and the probate of his estate is incomplete. That statement enabled me to get an extension on my tuition payments. Faced with the same predicament with tuition the following year, I reported that our rice crop failed due to drought and the probate of Dad's estate remained unresolved - another fabrication that extended my tuition payments. .

Irma and I married in December 1959 and hoped that our financial circumstance would change through our combined efforts. Unfortunately, her sponsoring hospital paid herself and other Caribbean nurses a fraction of the regular salary. The nurses, grateful for the sponsorship, accepted the wage offered. An exception, a Guyanese nurse sued the hospital for its unfair practice, and the court awarded her retroactive pay and the appropriate compensation. Her successful suit had no effect on the other nurses' wages. It would have if it were a class action suit. In spite of this and other challenges, Irma and I muddled through. However, I owed tuition upon graduation. To pay off the debt, I worked four jobs simultaneously for six months and sent payments to the college in installments. I slept on average three hours each night during that period. Short fifty cents on my final payment, the bursar sent me a note that he made up the difference.

My First Christmas

The first Christmas on campus in 1958 prior to my marriage in December 1959, Owen, Keith and I faced a bleak holiday, due to the lack of funds and no meal ticket. To survive, we asked other students in our dormitory to contribute to our hunger fund by donating their cupcakes and Twinkies they received at supper on Sundays. We placed a large brown paper bag at our doors in which they deposited them. Another part of our holiday diet consisted of black cake (made with lots of rum), rum and ginger beer sent to us by our parents in Guyana. Our all dessert diet (black cake, Twinkies, and cupcakes), combined with rum left us nauseous and inebriated. We thought how ironic that the cafeteria emptied gallons of milk in the drains and dumped a large amount of food daily and people everywhere in America, including us, goes hungry. Our friends Veatrice and Fred who lived close to the campus rescued us Christmas Eve by inviting us to spend Christmas day with them; we had an enjoyable time. However, the total dessert diet before and after the Christmas day meal had its toll. Owen, Keith and I broke out in large boils all over our bodies, which the college physician told us resulted from imbalanced nutrition.

Chapter Five
Driving in America

I arrived in America with a Guyanese driver's license. I desired an American driver's license, but obtaining one seemed unlikely without a car or funds to attend a driving school. I took a chance, however, and drove without one in spite of a major difference in the driving environment. In Guyana, motorists drove on the left and in America on the right. The adjustment turned out to be more difficult than I expected. Running low on beer at a party, I offered to purchase some more. The host offered her car to go to the store. Three women accompanied me to show the way. As I drove, they screamed for me to stay on the right-hand side of the road as I continually veered to the left facing oncoming traffic. When we arrived at the store, the women demanded the car keys so they could drive back to the party. They refused to let me drive in spite of my protestations. I gave in eventually. That incident occurred two months after I arrived in America, but as time went on and I drove with others, I became accustomed to driving on the right-hand side of the road.

Getting My Driver's License

Dependence on John, the only person with a driver's license in our group and his often inability or refusal to take us where we want to go, influenced my decision to hurry up and get my own. The following is an example: We visited a couple at their home in Cleveland Ohio, and everyone including John planned to drive to Warren Ohio the following morning to visit other friends. John canceled as we prepared to leave. Owen, Keith and I, angered by his abrupt decision, decided to drive ourselves without a license. We remained anxious throughout the trip and even abandoned our car when we saw a police roadblock ahead of us. We walked away from the car, returning to it after the roadblock cleared. We continued our trip and arrived at our destination without incident. We had a different experience on the return trip.

We got back to our friends' street in Cleveland without a problem, but could not find their house after driving up and down the street. Unable to find the house we became concerned. John had our friends' phone number, and we forgot to get it from him before we left. We never knew their last name. When we met the couple at the wife mother's home in Springfield Ohio, we introduced ourselves by first names. At their home, we continued to use first names.

We told a man at a gas station our plight, and he suggested that we might be on the wrong section of the street since a park separated its two sections. He agreed to take us to the section of street on the other side of the park. We followed him. He signaled for us to make a left turn when we got to the street. We made the turn as directed heading in the wrong direction into oncoming traffic of the one-way street. Panicked, we made an abrupt U-turn and pulled into a darkened area until a police car with a blaring siren passed. We continued on the street and found our friend's house.

A college mate offered to help me to get my American driver's license when I returned to campus. I passed the written driver's test and scheduled my road test. My college mate thought since I already knew to drive, I only needed to drive his car for a couple of hours to get the feel of it. He said on the day of my road test, I would drive his car for a while before we go for the road test. I never had the opportunity. On the day of the road test, my college mate picked me up in enough time to rush me to the test site. The inspector waited as we arrived. He got in the car and said, "Let's go." I just sat there. He looked at me and asked, "Is there a problem?" I did not respond, but I had a problem. It had begun to rain, and I had no idea how to turn on the windshield wipers. I acted as though tying my shoelace, all the while looking for the wiper control. I accidentally touched a button, and the wipers started, startling me. I put the car in gear, pressed the accelerator and gave the inspector and me such a whiplash it almost threw us in the back seat. The inspector shouted, "Stop!" He turned to me and asked, "Have you driven this car before?" I confessed, "No." He gestured for me to go. That time I pulled out gently. We drove a couple of blocks, and he told me to turn right. As I made the turn, he reached over and grabbed the steering wheel, his eyes bulging with fear. I slammed the brakes, and he let out a great sigh. Then he asked as he took a deep breath, "Didn't you see the parked car?" I said, "Yes, but I planned to turn away from it" I saw the car parked about fifty yards ahead as I made the right turn, but my classmate told me to make sure I made tight right turns. Obviously, the inspector thought I had turned too close for his comfort. We continued until I got to a traffic light. I stopped and waited for the red light to change. The inspector glanced at me, but I waited patiently until he asked, "Did you read the sign?" I looked up and had a sinking feeling. The sign indicated right turn permitted on red. I had sat waiting for the red light to change with no traffic in the vicinity. I could have made the turn a long time ago if I had read the sign. I continued to the station knowing I had flunked. As the inspector got out of the car, having given me my failing slip, he said, "Make sure you drive the car before you come back."

The next time I scheduled my road test I had familiarized myself with the car. My problem, no one to accompany me as the law required when driving with a learner's permit. I called the inspection station and asked if I could come in without a licensed driver. The woman on the phone told me I might take a chance; however, the officer might charge me and confiscate my car should I fail. I took the chance and passed the road test.

The 1948 Pontiac

Four of us (Keith, Owen, John and I) pooled funds and bought a car for sixty-five dollars, but had the challenge to keep it running. We had no money to buy antifreeze. We filled the radiator before leaving and drained it on our return. We bought gasoline half a gallon at a time (sixteen cents worth) restricting our driving to around the campus. We had the car for about a year before it came to its demise. Keith drove the car without adding water to the drained radiator causing it to catch fire. I recall him standing on campus with the car hood up and smoke spewing out. We sold it to a junkyard for ten dollars.

We drove the car, prior to its demise, to Cleveland Ohio summer of 1959, after mustering enough money to make the trip. A friend's son-in-law who lived there promised to introduce our calypso group to an entertainment promoter. On our way to Ohio, unfamiliar with the area we ended up on an isolated road. As I drove, darkness engulfed everything ahead in an unusual way. Alarmed, I hit the brakes hard waking my mates asleep in the car. I told them what I had observed, and we got out the car to investigate. It turned out the road had ended about fifty yards ahead and about to send us into an abyss. Someone had removed the barriers. The reality of what could have happened shook us, especially me. I trembled uncontrollably. It took an hour for me to calm down, in spite of my friends' effort to console me.

In Cleveland, we lost our way and ended up on a hilly two-lane road low on gasoline. To conserve gasoline, we applied what we termed "cruisematics" to conserve fuel. Using "cruisematics", we cut the engine at the top of a hill and cruised down. Looking back the action made no sense, but we felt good doing something about our predicament. In the end, the car ran out of gas. We had pushed it about two miles when we observed a farmhouse and decided to seek help. As four of us walked toward the house, one person shouted, "I see a gun!" and we dashed back through the gate toward the car. As we exited the yard, a car turned into the driveway. We continued to push the car when a young white male on a tractor pulled up behind us and said, "I brought you some gasoline." After filling our tank, he said he saw us pushing the car and concluded we might have run out of gasoline and needed help. He apologized for his mother's action. He said she pointed the gun because our presence scared her, especially alone at home. We expressed our appreciation for his help and continued on our way.

Chapter 6
Extraordinary Events

Unusual Experiences on Trips from College to New York City

A weekend trip with me, three other male students and a female student had an unexpected development. The trip took place during winter with lots of snow on the highway for the entire trip, which increased driving time from fourteen hours to nineteen hours. Along the way, we stopped five times for gasoline and bathroom facilities. The first couple of stops, everyone, got out except the female student. The males marveled at her endurance. Then the betting began. The males placed bets against each other on whether or when the female student would get out of the car. Would she get out at the next, the next or the next stop? Some of the males offer her tea and soda to increase their odds. She refused their offers and never got out the car the entire trip. They lost. When the female student got off at Penn Station in New York, one of the male students ran after her to see if she headed for a restroom. He lost sight of her ending the saga.

On another trip, a state trooper on the New Jersey turnpike pulled us over, three black males and two white females, for driving over the speed limit. He ordered us out of the car and threatened to take away the driver's license. The male driver and the other males got out and stood with the trooper while he berated us for speeding and endangering other motorists. As the trooper continued to speak, his gaze shifted to the ground beside the car. One of the white female students rolled out the car clutching her stomach, writhing in pain, moaning and groaning. The trooper continued to admonish the driver but glanced periodically at the female student on the ground. Her groans grew louder and louder, and we all became concerned that she had a serious acute illness. The trooper asked, "What's wrong with her?" We shrugged our shoulders. Her pains seemed to become more and more severe. We gathered around the student on the ground as the other female student consoled her. The trooper worried, by his expression, asked, "Should I call an ambulance?" The female student attending to the ailing student said, "No, she would be alright if we hurry!" The trooper said, "O.K., get going!" Surprised that he let us go, we took off in a hurry still worried about our friend until she began to laugh. She had faked her illness unknown to us. Her performance deserved an Oscar.

Scheme to Get Cheap Car Rides to New York

Irma and I established a home in Brooklyn, New York after marriage in December 1959 (my sophomore year) because many of her fellow Guyanese nurses and other friends lived in New York and New Jersey. I came home from college in Ohio as often as our budget allowed. The steepness of fares, however, limited my trips. I came up with a scheme that would allow me to travel home more often if it worked. I offered college mates who drove to and from New York or Connecticut, some weekends, to undertake the driving both ways for a twenty-five dollar fare. Several of them accepted my offer. After the first trip under my agreement, I took three days to recuperate missing a few classes. I resolved, however, to continue to make the trips. Halfway to New York on my second trip, I dozed off for a few seconds; the car swerved, waking the students. I told the student who owned the car, I needed to pull off the road and sleep a couple of hours before continuing. He thought my request ridiculous. How can I ask to sleep for two hours on a weekend trip? He insisted I continue driving to fulfill our arrangement. The other students would have none of it. They asked him how I could drive if I am tired. The owner and another student drove the rest of the way to New York where I got off, and they continued to Connecticut. I drove back to campus on the return trip. After that experience, halfway to New York on each weekend trip under the same arrangement with different car owners, I made the same maneuver and complained that I need to pull over and sleep, with the same results. The car owner and another student took over and drove the rest of the way. The practice helped me to recuperate in a day or two rather than three days after a trip.

A couple years after I had made weekend trips with five different car owners, a group of us students gathered in a dorm room on a bull session and the subject of the New York trips came up. One car owner asked, "Could you imagine that on our way to New York for a weekend, Eric wants to pull over and sleep for two hours?" In response, the other four car owners chimed in, "He did that to you? He pulled that stunt on me!" That ended my little scheme. Fortunately, I had only a few months to graduation and no need to rely on the ride

The Diarrhea Incident

On campus, one evening at eleven thirty, my roommate and I had recently turned into bed when he complained of abdominal cramps. I knew that he received an oral smallpox vaccine earlier in the day and suggested that that might have caused his discomfort. A couple hours later, my roommate responded to a knock on our door. Upon opening it, a student snatched our trash pail just inside the door and took off. My roommate and I stepped into the hallway and saw students running helter-skelter. Students wrestled in the bathroom trying to get to a commode. One student defecated in the slop sink; others headed out the dormitory trying to find somewhere to relieve themselves. Pandemonium reigned everywhere. As my roommate and I looked out the dormitory, someone shouted, "The gym is open," and female students in their nightgowns from different dormitories headed in its direction. So far, my roommate and I had suffered no discomfort, but the situation changed soon after and we had to find a bathroom fast. Luckily, things had calmed down somewhat allowing us to find one, albeit in a mess.

By late morning, the ninety-nine percent of students in my dormitory who had succumbed to the diarrhea attack stood in line for a dose of Kaopectate in the housemother's office. At the same time, two lines formed at the cafeteria for breakfast. The line of students affected by the diarrhea attack snaked around the building; the line for those unaffected had a handful of students. In the cafeteria, a group of female students stood in line ahead of me chatting. One of them shifted her weight from one leg to the other while grimacing. After going through the motions for a few minutes, she made a sudden dash for the bathroom. After a few steps, she stopped, clinched her fists – arms held over her head as she contorted her body. She froze in that position for few seconds, before dashing to the bathroom with her friends in tow. They remained in the bathroom for quite some time, while some friends got a change of clothing from her room.

The college administration suspected salmonella poisoning from the chicken potpie served by the cafeteria and consumed by the majority of students the previous evening. The reason for the campus-wide diarrhea episode remains a mystery, however, because of inconclusive laboratory test results.

My Trip to Louisville, Kentucky

A college mate asked me to hitchhike with him to his aunt (Aunt) and uncle's (Uncle) home in Kentucky during spring break. We left the first day of spring break. A friend's parents who came to pick him up gave us a ride to the main highway on the outskirts of Cincinnati close to their home. We stood on the highway for about an hour when a car stopped and offered us a ride. We introduced ourselves to the driver and his friend. On our way, my friend and the driver discovered their family ties (cousins). My friend's cousin lived in Kentucky and took us to their Aunt and Uncle's home. Although grateful for the ride all the way to our destination, I had jitters throughout the trip. My friend and his cousin, having discovered their kinship, chatted all the way. At the same time, the driver sped, gesticulated and paid little attention to the road.

We enjoyed our stay in Kentucky where I got my first shoeshine. On our way to an event at the University of Kentucky, my friend's Uncle stopped for a shoe shine and invited me to have one. At the movies, I had seen people on the street shining other people's shoes as a business, and wondered why someone left his home with dirty shoes to have someone else clean them.

Uncle introduced me to bootleg (corn) whiskey. We stopped

at a little bar, and he got two bottles of the stuff. He asked if I had corn whiskey before and I shook my head, no. He whipped out some plastic cups and poured some for each of the four of us. We arrived at the University a short while after and as I stepped out the car, my knees buckled. Everyone had a good laugh. I prided myself to take a stiff drink. As a pharmacist in Guyana, I compounded with high proof alcohol and often would take a drink.

My mate from college and his date, another couple and I went to a nightclub for an evening out. The DJ played beautiful music, but I had come without a partner. A beautiful woman sat across the room, and I started to go over and ask her for a dance. I had made two steps when my friend grabbed my arm and pulled me back. He suggested I stay and dance with the two women in our party. The women also chimed in that I should stay and dance with them. Their rationale puzzled me, but as a guest, I acquiesced. Leaving the nightclub at three o'clock in the morning, my friend said he wanted to show me something. As we drove slowly, he pulled up alongside the woman I wanted to dance with; she stood under a lamplight. My friend said, "Take a look!" The woman turned out to be a man with a pronounced shadow on his face. His beard had grown. My friends had discouraged me from asking the woman to dance because they recognized the person as a male in spite of his makeup.

We returned to his Aunt and Uncle's home about four-thirty that morning. Uncle sat on a sofa with swollen eyes and bruises on his face. Wrapped in a thick blanket and in pain, he must have been in a fight, we thought. We had our suspicion, but he never answered our questions as to what had happened. Later, he mumbled to his wife that he was in a fight to assuage her anger, but gave no details.

Aunt went shopping the next day. That is when Uncle told us what had happened. We drank wine as he explained. He met a woman at a nightclub and offered to take her home. On the way, they began to make out in the car. When the woman turned out to be a man, he got angry and punched him. In turn, Uncle got a whipping.

My friend's Aunt cooked tasty food and we gorged ourselves. The morning of our departure, we thanked Aunt and Uncle for their hospitality and headed out to the highway to hitchhike back to campus. It took two hours in freezing weather before we got a ride to Cincinnati. We rode a bus across town to a highway heading toward campus, and soon after got a ride with a college mate's parents taking him back to campus.

Visiting a Friend in New York City

I arrived on Sunday night the week of Thanksgiving. That night as we talked about old times and our studies, my friend told me we had to leave his apartment by seven o'clock in the morning to avoid the landlord; he owed him a couple months' rent. Falling behind in his studies, he gave up one of his jobs resulting in the delinquency. He awaited funds from a recent scholarship to bring his rent current. The first three mornings of my stay, we left his apartment at six-thirty, had breakfast at a deli and either toured the city or went to the library, before returning in the evening.

Friday morning, the day after Thanksgiving, I left his apartment at six o'clock with another friend. My friend, still in bed, told us he would leave soon. On our way back to the apartment in the early afternoon, a fire engine stood with lights flashing behind my friend's building. Concerned, we pushed our way through the crowd gathered to get a better view of the proceedings. We followed everyone's gaze and looked up as a firefighter moved up his ladder toward a balcony where someone stood in underpants and shirtless. The firefighter shouted as he climbed, "Don't jump!" We recognized the person on the balcony as my friend as we drew near. It made no sense why he would stand on his balcony almost naked, uncharacteristic of him.

We rushed to his apartment to find out what had happened. A couple of firefighters and the landlord argued as we entered the apartment. The landlord defended himself against the firefighters' charge that he endangered our friend's life. We surmised what had happened, although without the facts. Later we found out that our friend had overslept, heard the landlord using his spare key to enter the apartment and went out on the balcony. He thought he would survive the cold in his underpants for a few minutes. He reasoned that the landlord would leave immediately in his absence. Instead, the landlord sat on his bed and made notes. As soon as my friend had stepped onto the balcony outside his window, someone called the fire department fearing an attempted suicide. The fire station a block away responded immediately. My friend said when he heard the fire engine he tried to locate the fire. He never thought himself the subject of interest.

The Burning Hair

I attended a conference in Kerhonkson, New York. An evening at supper, I sat at a table with nine white women. After supper, we told stories about having a good time. The woman next to me, a great storyteller, lit a match but rather than light her cigarette she paused to emphasize a point with the lit match at head level. In a flash her thinning hair went up in flames; I reacted by dousing her hair with a mug of water on the table. The other guests at the table gazed at her stupefied by her hair afire and my reaction. The woman unaware of what had occurred looked at me with disdain and attacked me. The woman in the adjacent seat grabbed her as the other women shouted in unison, "He saved your life!" I understood the woman's embarrassment and discomfort from the soaking but thought she over-reacted by attacking me before inquiring the reason for my action. Would she have reacted that way if I were white? The question remains unresolved in my mind. The woman did apologize for her overreaction and thank me for my prompt action.

An Embarrassing Moment

In Massachusetts, a friend offered me a ride home but had to pick up his girlfriend on the way. When we got to her home, I got in the back seat as he went upstairs to fetch his girlfriend. His girlfriend's mother welcomed my friend at the door, and as they engaged in conversation, his girlfriend slipped passed them without acknowledging him and headed for the car. She opened the car door and as she flopped herself in the front passenger seat let out a long, loud and obnoxious fart fanning furiously to dissipate the odor through the door, left open. She sensed someone in the back seat, spun around and stared at me in disbelief. I said, "Hello, my name is Eric" meeting her for the first time. Visibly shaken by my presence, she took a deep breath and managed to get out her name. We laughed. My friend came back to the car and inquired if we had met. We nodded and smiled at each other. I never betrayed his girlfriend's secret.

The Suckling Pig

While, in Massachusetts, I decided to barbecue a suckling pig for my friends from New York – a bad idea, as it turned out. The pig arrived from the butcher dressed with an apple in its mouth on a fancy tray. As I looked at it, my mouth watered in anticipation of the taste of tender, succulent meat. I placed the carcass on the grill and started the rotisserie. I watched for what seemed an eternity as fat dripped, and dripped and dripped; the carcass decreased in size with little meat in sight. I knew that a suckling pig would have more fat than muscle, but the minimal amount of meat on that carcass surprised me. Meanwhile, the friends from New York teased me chanting in unison, "We want barbecue pork." Embarrassed standing in front of the grill with my chef's hat and apron, my wife Irma saved the day by ordering and preparing other meats.

Chapter Seven
Food

My Guyanese nomenclature of foods caused embarrassing moments. I look forward to the purchase of a ball of cheese wrapped in a red outer coating, similar to my favorite cheese in Guyana, as I enter a cheese store. I asked the clerk for a Dutchman head. The store went silent, as the clerk and customers stared at me. I walked over and picked up one of the balls of cheese. I heard a big sigh throughout the store, and the clerk exclaimed, "Oh Gouda!" A very popular cheese at Christmas in Guyana, everyone knew it as Dutchman head – the name likely came from its country of origin and shape.

Another embarrassing moment came when I asked for ice-apple in a market. The clerk told me with a smirk, "We grow apples; we don't make them from ice." The term made sense in Guyana. We called foreign apples "ice-apples" because they came packed in ice. We also differentiated them from the local apples – golden apple, star apple, monkey apple and custard apple.

I had to acquaint myself with the way merchants packaged foods and sold produce. Unaware that shopkeepers sold chicken by parts because my Mom reared her own in Guyana, I endured an embarrassing moment. In New York, a Guyanese friend invited me to dinner. On arrival, the host and other friends at the dinner told me to help myself to the curry chicken and other dishes on the stove. I dipped into a large pot of curry. To my surprise, the spoon had about six gizzards on it. Setting aside the first spoonful, I dipped into the curry chicken again. Once more, I came up with about the same number of gizzards. I surmised that my friend cooked many chickens since one gizzard came from each chicken. I thought how inconsiderate of my friends to leave me only gizzards when my friend cooked so many chickens. I stepped out the kitchen and berated my friends that they should be ashamed of themselves for leaving me only gizzards. In unison, everyone responded, "Eat the damn gizzard curry and be grateful." I realized then that my friend had cooked gizzard curry.

Restaurants prepared certain foods different to my experience. In Guyana, the Chinese restaurants prepared Chow Mein and Lo Mein with soft noodles. Chow Mein contained short noodles and Lo Mein long noodles. The first time I ordered Chow Mein in New York City, it came with crisp noodles. Surprised, I thought the restaurant sent a wrong order. Restaurants in Guyana seasoned their hamburgers before cooking them. In America, seeing a hamburger patty placed on a grill from a package surprised me.

Armed with the knowledge that stores sold chicken parts, I invited Owen and Keith to dinner. I cooked curried chicken wings and rice. Cooking the rice, my next room neighbor sitting in the kitchen told me I needed to turn down the flame. I thought her suggestion unnecessary because I had "cooked rice" before in Guyana – a place known for its long grain rice. To my surprise when I lifted the pot cover after boiling the rice for about twenty minutes, the pot contained one big glob that looked like starch. I ran to the trash bin to see if I inadvertently bought starch. Seeing the label on the packet "minute rice" floored me, I had never heard of such a thing. When Owen and Keith arrived, I served the curry wings with bread. They stared at me and asked what happened to the rice. To hide my ignorance, I told them my budget precluded the purchase of rice. I came clean with them about my foul-up with the minute rice, weeks later.

I continued to be as frugal as possible, although I realized the futility of trying to save enough money to pay tuition from my meager wages. I took my lunch to work at the warehouse where Owen, Keith and I worked, until Keith had the brilliant idea that I should credit my lunch, as he did, from the delicatessen across the street. Sticker shock awaited me when I received my first bill for ten dollars. I found the amount of the bill too high for lunch with a weekly paycheck of thirty-two dollars and a rent of seventeen dollars; I also needed to save for tuition. My adventure into Delicatessen lunches lasted one week. I went back to brown bagging.

Owen, Keith and I lived together and shared the grocery bill. I cooked all meals. Although I had cooked only once in Guyana, I observed my Mom cooking and found that the task came easily to me. As a result, Owen and Keith convinced me to do the cooking, and they would assist. I accepted. They helped with peeling and chopping ingredients as I directed. Our arrangement worked well for a while. One afternoon after returning from work, they watched baseball while I cooked without their assistance. The pattern continued the next day. The following day, without complaint, I cooked a single serving for myself, ate, washed and stored the dishes. Keith and Owen smelled the food and came to find out when dinner would be ready. They gazed at the stove, void of pots and pans, and asked what happened to the food. When I told them what I had done, they stomped out the kitchen visibly upset. I asked them how they expect dinner without offering their assistance. I disliked the action I took because of our close friendship, but it served me well. I could be more frugal without the constraint that existed under our previous arrangement, where each of us ate and drank without consideration for the others. We dissolved our arrangement; Owen and Keith took care of their own groceries and cooking. Our relationship suffered for a week before returning to normal.

Summer time, ten or more fellow students visited Irma and me on weekends. Irma cooked a large pot of "cook-up rice"- a dish made of rice combined with meats and vegetables. Eating the food, however, involved an unusual process – eating in relay. Our home had two plates and two spoons; therefore, we ate two persons at a time; the last couple to eat had the choice of eating out of the pot and its cover. Folks suggest we could have solved the utensil shortage by purchasing paper plates. As students for whom every penny counted, we considered such purchases a waste of money.

John, Owen, Keith and I lived together summer of 1959 in Springfield, Ohio. We shared expenses for food and rent. John never contributed to the purchase of food but ate leftovers from our cooking. However, he bought fruits and honey that he claimed helpful to preserve his voice as the lead singer of our calypso group. Keith ate one of his bananas and John became belligerent; he warned us never to touch his fruit. His behavior incensed me; I, therefore, ate his remaining four bananas as he ranted and raved about the one Keith had eaten, daring him to stop me when he had eaten our leftover meals for several weeks. John glared at me but said nothing. Thereafter, we forbade him from eating our leftovers.

Keith loved linked sausages. He cooked them almost daily. One night, as he cooked his sausages over a high flame, we suggested that he turned down the heat. He dismissed our caution asserting that he knew how to cook. Within seconds, his sausages caught fire and burnt to a crisp. As we shook our heads at the charcoal in the pan, Keith in typical fashion passed his hand over his head and said, "I like my sausages well done!" and ate them. Every time something went wrong because of Keith's action, he proclaimed it perfect. Like the time, he had a friend cut his hair because he refused to wait for me to cut it the next day. His haircut had chunks the size of nickels and dimes gouged out all over. His haircut looked awful, but in typical fashion, Keith proclaimed it just the way he liked it. He knew he had a bad haircut because the next day he asked me to correct the flaws.

Chapter Eight
Racial and Cultural Challenges

I knew nothing about Jim Crow or apartheid prior to coming to America. I arrived during the civil rights movement and its many sit-ins. In Xenia, (Ohio) a restaurant refused to serve blacks. Keith, Owen and I joined other Central State College and Antioch College students and picketed around it. No sit-ins occurred, because the owner closed the restaurant. We hesitated to join the picketing at first because several individuals told us that as foreign students the House of Un-American Activities would deport us. After some thought, we concluded that we had to participate to stop the un-American activities of the restaurant owner. We marveled that most occasions whites picketed without any blacks among them. That observation gave us greater impetus to participate. Dr. Martin Luther King's commencement speech at Central State college that year (1959) strengthened our resolve to participate in the demonstrations.

At college during civil right activities in 1959, I pondered the difference in race relations between Guyana and America. As America, Guyana has a multiracial population. People of African (Blacks) and East Indian (Indians) descent dominated the population, with smaller numbers of Britons, Chinese, Portuguese, Aborigines and others. Each group had a distinct existence. I grew up in Guyana under colonial rule, and the Britons held the top public service positions and the governorship. Blacks came to Guyana as slaves and the East Indians as indentured servants. The other nationalities immigrated to Guyana. The Aborigines are the original inhabitants. As slaves, Blacks worked in the sugar industry and the Indians as indentured servants in rice production. After emancipation from slavery, Blacks adopted the British way of life. Stripped of their African heritage as slaves, without a common religion or language, they had no choice. They pursued education with great zeal and became part of the learned and professional classes. The Indians with British approval retained their languages and religions and maintained contact with India their country of origin. They received continual counsel from that government.

Blacks rose to the highest positions in the civil service permitted by the British, and became lawyers, nurses, doctors and other professionals; very few pursued business. On the other hand, circumstances restricted Indians to business. They remained in rice production, which restricted them from working regular 8 a.m. to 4 p.m. (9 to 5 in the United States) jobs. They needed the flexibility to devote time to cultivate and harvest rice crops. Owning their businesses allowed them at those times to put the majority of adults and children to work, leaving a small number to run the businesses. The majority of Indian children stayed away from school during those periods. Indians emphasized earning and saving money to return to India. In 1953, many Indians returned to India in chartered ships. Treated as low caste upon arrival, they returned to Guyana and became involved in all aspects of Guyanese life; they had the resources to do so. A bank, with Portuguese in all middle and upper management positions, replaced its Portuguese tellers within six months with Indians to get their deposits.

Tensions rose as East Indians entered fields traditionally held by Blacks, which resulted in race riots. The Chinese and Portuguese are fewer in number than Blacks and Indians; they work in the civil service and businesses. Guyanese society, as in America, has marginalized the Aborigines - the original inhabitants of the country who struggle to maintain their identity or enjoy the benefits of the country's resources.

Our family never experienced racial hostilities. Of course, favoritism existed among the groups. Growing up, the interaction between the ethnic groups had been limited and without friction. I mostly had Black teachers throughout my education in Guyana, with one each of Indian, Portuguese, and Chinese ethnicity.

Coming from a society based on social class, I had difficulty accepting that an uneducated and poor white man in America felt superior to all black men, irrespective of their education and self-worth. The experience of Owen and Dr. Lee, our college physician, illustrates the phenomenon. Dr. Lee and Owen driving on a highway in Ohio observed a car veer off the highway into a ravine. Dr. Lee decided to stop to offer his assistance if needed. One of the two white men who reeked of alcohol had a deep laceration on his forehead that bled profusely. Dr. Lee offered to suture the wound, and the man agreed. The man's groans during the procedure caused his friend to ask him to act like a white man and stop groaning in front of the niggers. Owen deduced the men had little formal education from the way they expressed themselves, which upset him because the men acted as though entitled to Dr. Lee's help. According to Owen, the man helped by Dr. Lee muttered an almost inaudible thank you. Hearing about the incident, I realized that once the US constitution stated that a black man equals three-fifths of a white man, that declaration made such an indelible impression on the white American psyche that it would take a very long time, if ever, for whites in America to accept blacks as their equal.

At Columbia University, many of my white classmates my age already had ten or more years of experience in our field of epidemiology. They called themselves re-treads. Employed without advanced degrees, they gained knowledge and experience through on the job training. They returned to university to consolidate their advantage by obtaining academic credentials. The number of white television news anchors and radio hosts without a college education or previous work experience get opportunities to prove themselves while employers turned away talented blacks with multiple advanced degrees for lack of experience. I faced the same obstacle during my career. On two occasions, human resource executives told me that decision makers would reject my application because I pose a threat. I never could imagine what threat I posed. My experiences mirrored those of Supreme Court justices Clarence Thomas and Sonia Sotomayor, who intimated that employers looked askance at their hard work to graduate from a top university. I had a rewarding career, in spite of limitations. I, therefore, urge every student to go after his education with resolve. Education helps to assure a purposeful life.

As recent as the 1970s, the medical profession limited the advancement of black physicians. As a health care administrator in Central Harlem, NY, I observed first-hand the frustrations of black physicians. Most of them worked in government jobs such as school health, social disease, and child health clinics; some of them had small practices without hospital privileges in most instances. In Harlem, the fortunate few black physicians had admitting privileges at public institutions, Harlem and Sydenham hospitals, and two small private hospitals owned by black physicians - Matthews and Cavanaugh. A physician friend of mine, an ophthalmologist, had hospital privileges at a major white-run hospital. He told me that none of his white colleagues acknowledged him in the hospital, not even in the physician lounge as they prepared for surgery. I knew two black physicians who drank heavily in their frustration.

Public financing of health care (Medicare, Medicaid, New York City Ghetto Medicine Program, etc.) expanded opportunities for black physicians to affiliate with white-run hospitals that wanted to attract black patients to improve their bottom line. White-run hospitals flourished, and black physicians enhanced their practices, but black- run hospitals suffered a setback. The American system for grading hospitals exalted the white-run hospitals to prestige status; consequently, black patients with their newfound opportunity clamored for the white-run hospitals. Black physicians trained at black medical schools have great difficulty persuading their black patients to utilize services offered by their alma mater. In some instances, the shift in patient preference has reduced the varied morbidities at black hospitals endangering their ability to support certain residencies, necessitating their affiliation with white-run hospitals.

As a secretary of one of the YMCA branches in Guyana from age 14, I came to America with a letter of introduction to the New York City branch. I wrote to the branch and enclosed my letter of introduction. They responded wishing me well with my studies and suggested I visit a Presbyterian church in Xenia Ohio that matched my religious affiliation in Guyana. As suggested, I met Reverend Darling at the church; he welcomed me with great enthusiasm and expressed his desire to have me inform the youth in the church about my country. After his warm welcome, he went on to explain that some elderly congregants might give me a cold shoulder. According to him, they adhere to the teaching that Negros descended from Ham whom God cursed, which forbade Negroes and whites from worshipping together. He went on to say that, things have changed, and whites and blacks could worship together. I listened then asked who lifted God's curse. Reverend Darling hesitated to respond; I told him I reject the change as arbitrary unless someone in the church convinces me that God removed the curse. Otherwise, the church could re-impose the curse on blacks at its whim excluding us once more. I returned the church literature he had given me, wished him well and left after his inability to convince me that God had lifted the curse.

I had a disconcerting experience with a white roommate (a veteran), from which I learned temperance. We had a confrontation the first night that I moved in. The administration reassigned me to his room after they condemned my previous dormitory. We argued over a window. He slept on the bed next to the radiator under the window and insisted that the window remain open. I found leaving the window open on a cold winter's night unacceptable, especially with the cold air blowing directly at my bed on the opposite side of the room. Each of us insisted on having his way. He opened the window; I closed it. We continued that way for about an hour. I closed the window once more; he left it closed. Instead, he took two revolvers from a drawer and placed them on his desk. I took out the scalpel from my dissecting kit and placed it on my desk. Seeing the two revolvers, I told my roommate to make sure I die if he attempts to hurt me, or I would find him and destroy him. Without responding, he opened the window once more, and I closed it. So it continued until morning. He opened the window. I closed it. Later in the morning, I reported to the dean's office that my roommate displayed two guns during our argument. They confiscated his guns. The next night the window remained closed, but we never spoke. The following Sunday before I left for the cafeteria, I offered to bring back some food for him. He had a meal ticket but never went to the cafeteria on Sundays. He detested dressing up; he wore khaki shirt and pants daily, changed underwear three or four times a day and wore wooden clogs barefooted, even in winter. I brought back cookies and fruit for him. Thereafter, our relationship thawed slowly until it improved to the point that we decided to room together the next semester. The opportunity never materialized because my roommate died in an accident a few days before I returned to campus the next semester. A car struck him as he ran to town. An avid long distance runner, he ran daily. One morning he invited me for a short run – eight miles. I declined politely.

My interaction with white female students at Antioch College in the late 1950s illustrated the lack of interaction between blacks and whites. Several students (mostly southerners) asked to touch my hair to experience its texture; they told me they had never been in the company of a black male, due to parental restrictions. Asking to touch my hair reminded me of my brother's experience in London, England in 1951. Young white children rubbed his arm to see if the black pigment came off. Suspicion and misinformation abound within blacks and whites, fostered by those who benefit from the division, which continues to hamper relations. Students asked me about head-hunters in my country. Responding, I joked that I knew nothing about head- hunting preferring the body myself.

Conversations with white female students confirmed my view that anyone with a goal takes steps to avoid pitfalls that might derail it. For example, several white female students at Antioch College told me they came to college fitted with contraceptive diaphragms. In 1969, as a student in a Manpower class at Columbia University, the professor discussed how farm girls decide whether to become sexually active. Girls with no intention of pursuing higher education or leave home to seek opportunities elsewhere became sexually active at a young age, many starting families; girls with expanded ambitions refrained from doing so. I believe that the same reasoning applies to girls in low- income black communities with a high incidence of teenage pregnancy. Many of the young women who become pregnant at a young age have no ambitions beyond their present circumstance due to imposed limitations on them. Consequently, they have no reason to postpone sexual activity.

The knowledge that youth who establish personal goals avoid situations that deter their attainment gave me the impetus to participate as an instructor in an abstinence program,

REACH, under the auspices of the Department of Family

Medicine, at the University of Maryland, School of Medicine. The program helped vulnerable youth between the ages of 9 and 14 avoid early pregnancy by delaying sexual activity. As part of the program, students performed laboratory experiments under the supervision of graduate students from the science departments of the University of Maryland at Baltimore. We hoped to peek the students' interest in science to encourage them to place more emphasis on their studies in the hope of pursuing scientific careers. I have no idea if any of the students pursued science because of their exposure, but most of the program participants avoided pregnancy - concentrating on their studies.

Quite a few students at Central State College had a perverse view of other countries. Owen, Keith and I placed ginger root and water in large glass jars to make ginger beer – a popular Guyanese beverage. Students, who visited our rooms and saw the ginger floating in jars, assumed that we used the concoction for nefarious purposes. Consequently, word got around that Keith, Owen and I practiced witchcraft and could harm people. Keith took advantage of his newfound reputation to get his way in the recreation room. An avid Wyatt Earp fan, he walked into the T.V. lounge and changed the channel from a baseball game to his Wyatt Earp program, without asking permission from the student watching the show. The student protested until Keith turned to him and said, "I'll make you fly!" The student walked away without another word, which dumbfounded me. Keith got away with it!

Our group encountered unusual behaviors when we visited the home of the wealthy couple responsible for the creation of our calypso group. They lived in an exclusive suburb of Cincinnati and paid our cab fare to their home. Cab drivers when given their address inquired if our mothers worked there. One night the couple told us the paperboy would take us home instead of calling a cab. An elderly black man, possibly in his sixty, smoking a cigar pulled up to the curb in a Cadillac automobile. We thought it incredulous that such caring people would debase the personage of an elderly black man in that manner. On our visits, the couple frolicked with us except in the presence of our black American friends. They became less animated.

We pondered their change in behavior but never came up with a credible explanation.

John had a peculiar relationship with whites. He realized that the greater his aloofness toward them, the harder they tried to win his affection. Yet, he liked to associate with whites. He dated white girls exclusively and married one of them. His experiences as an ordained minister in America prior to attending Central State College might have influenced his response to whites.

An incident that occurred when we spent a spring recess at the home of a Presbyterian minister and his wife illustrates the difficulty whites had trying to fathom John's behavior. John received an invitation from the couple and asked their permission to bring Keith, Owen and me. They agreed. After a hearty welcome upon our arrival, they gave John keys to a station wagon and a credit card for gasoline during our stay. Owen, Keith and I slept at a congregant's home and went back to the minister's home in the morning; John stayed at the minister's home. The first morning at breakfast the minister invited us to his church's sunrise service to occur the following Sunday. The Saturday prior to the sunrise service John announced that he had no intention of attending; the minister's expression showed his disappointment. Later that day in John's absence, the minister urged us to influence John to attend. Four-thirty in the morning on the day of the service, I called the minister's home and asked him to get John to the telephone. When John answered, I pleaded with him to go to the sunrise service, but he declined. He became indignant when told that the minister had asked us to encourage him to attend the service. After hanging up the phone, he asked the minister if he thought he had the right to insist that he attend the sunrise service because he stayed at his home. Owen, Keith and I attended the sunrise service and almost froze because of our flimsy clothing. After the service, everyone went to the church for breakfast. As we sat, John sauntered in and had his breakfast. In spite of John's actions, the minister and his wife continued to pamper him throughout the remainder of our stay.

The couple (benefactors of our calypso group) visited us on campus to discuss a matter concerning the calypso group. They arranged to meet us on a Sunday at 3:30 in the afternoon. Everyone, except John, arrived at the meeting place on time. Two hours later, John, the leader of our group remained absent. He came at 5:45 p.m. When asked if he had forgotten our appointment with the couple, he replied that he had important business to conduct. He continued further to say that, the couple wanted to see him and should have had no problem waiting. The wife became distraught and sobbed as her husband comforted her with a hug as she questioned her ability to get John to respond to her efforts in a more positive manner stating, "I don't know why I can't reach him." We concluded the meeting, and they left.

At the dormitory the next morning, the wife called for John. I answered because he had left for class. She insisted that one of the other members of our group receive a package she sent to John, special delivery. Her insistence that one of us stick around to receive her gift to John incensed me; since the only gift I received from her had been a second-hand pair of shoes from her son. The shoes, a size B while I wore a size D, caused me great pain and embarrassment. I wore the shoes to escort a female college mate to an international dinner on campus. I took them off at the function because my feet hurt. I had to walk my date to her dormitory barefooted. The pavement tore my socks. Embarrassed I let the young lady walk into her dormitory alone. John received his package from the office when he returned to the dormitory. It contained a dozen tab collar shirts - the latest fashion. Each shirt cost forty dollars at that time. We marveled how John manipulated whites to get the best out of them.

At a summer job in 1958, I observed how my employer prejudged a young black man seeking employment. I worked in a small cap factory in New York pressing the caps by placing wooden blocks in them and applying steam to keep their shape. One day my boss called me into the front area where he cut fabric in different patterns for the caps. He told me I seemed intelligent enough to assist him to put the large pieces of cloth in layers; the other young black and Hispanic employees, according to him, lacked the capacity to do so. I believed, however, that anyone in the shop could have helped him with the simple task. As we cut the fabric, a young black man neatly dressed walked in and inquired about a job, in perfect English. My boss dismissed him without hesitation, stating he had no positions available. After the young man had left, he turned to me and asked, "How can you apply for a job smoking a cigar?" referring to the small unlit cigar the young man held between his fingers. The shop had vacancies; we had discussed earlier the need to hire additional workers. I also knew that the available jobs required no special skills.

In Massachusetts, I encountered police bias. A fellow student and I had a car accident around 2:00 a.m. at an intersection. The traffic light had turned green, and as I moved forward across the intersection, the car to my right ran the red light, struck my car and spun it around. Two white women emerged from their vehicle and came over to check on us. As we spoke, a squad car drove up; one of the police officers without asking any questions said to me, "You ran the red light and almost killed these women." Astonished, I asked the police officer how he came to his conclusion since he arrived after the accident. He told me never mind and wrote me a ticket for running a red light.

As a student new to Massachusetts in 1968, I asked a couple of my professors if they knew of an attorney who could represent me for a traffic ticket. They referred me to the law school. I met with an attorney there who insisted that I pay him up front to represent me, stating that he offer no guarantees. I turned down his counsel and decided to represent myself. I appeared in court with a diagram of the accident scene and a couple of toy cars from my five-year-old son, ready to defend myself. The prosecutor read the charge against me. The judge then asked if I had any questions for the charging officer who stood in the box before me. I asked the officer if he recalls what he said to me when he arrived at the scene of the accident. Before the officer could respond, the judge leaned forward and said, "You mean you did not see the accident occur." When the officer responded he did not, the judge told the prosecutor he had better quit while still ahead. He dismissed the case.

I faced housing discrimination when I looked for an apartment to begin graduate studies at Brandeis University. A Jewish friend, Joel, accompanied me to Waltham, Massachusetts a weekend to look for an apartment before I commenced classes. We saw an advertisement for an apartment close to the University. Joel called, and the homeowner confirmed the availability of the lower apartment of her house. I arrived at the residence five minutes later, and the owner told me she had rented it. Next, we responded to an advertisement for a room to let. An elderly white man answered the door and escorted us to the room for let, closing each room door before we passed. I liked the room, but his demeanor made me uncomfortable and apprehensive about living there. I decided to continue my search. .

I asked the next owner I spoke to if she would have a problem renting to a black foreign student. She told me no and invited me to go to see the unit. Joel and I arrived at the house before her. We stood in the yard as she arrived and introduced herself. She asked us to follow as she began to climb the stairs. Soused, she struggled to keep her balance as she ascended the stairs. When she raised her foot, it seemed to take forever to land on the next tread as she swayed with one arm in the air to keep her balance. The second floor had two bedrooms - one occupied by two middle-aged white men and the other vacant. Occupants shared the bathroom. I rented the room on a month-to-month basis but regretted my decision soon after. The two men in the adjacent room stayed drunk. They remained in their room except to stagger across the road on Saturday to replenish their stash of liquor. They threw their empty liquor bottles on the floor in their room and in the hallway. I shuddered to use the bathroom the way they kept it dirty, in spite of my efforts to keep it clean. I lent them my iron and ironing board; they fell asleep with the iron plugged in face down on the ironing board causing it to catch fire. I had to enter their room, always open and unplug the iron. I vacated my room after two months.

Next, I moved to Natick, Massachusetts - a white community. My wife and our two children joined me six months later. We had a new experience as the only Black family. The first day of school my children, Denise, and Dane, stood in front of our house awaiting the school bus. When it arrived, and Denise saw a bus filled with white children, she ran into the house. The children had no effect on Dane, who kept calling Denise to get on the bus.

Dane started school in the second half of the first grade and Denise the third as the only black children in the school. We enrolled Denise in the third grade because her previous school groomed her to skip the second grade by placing her in a one-month accelerated second-grade class. Initially, Denise had difficulty keeping up with her schoolwork but at the end of the term, she and Dane had mastered their studies and read three levels above their grade. They earned scholarships to attend a summer enrichment program at Harvard University.

We rented a house in Natick from Dr. Loomis, one of my professors. He and his wife had invited Irma and me to spend a weekend. They had great wealth – a mansion with all the amenities, including tennis courts. As we sat on their porch enjoying a cocktail, I admired their manicured lawn. Dr. Loomis suggested I check it out. I touched it and discovered artificial grass. They had great influence in their community. Mrs. Loomis saved the day for us when our furnishings arrived from New York. The truck driver refused to unload the truck and would have charged us for the additional time our furnishings remained unloaded from the truck unless we paid by cash or a certified check. We had a personal check. The moving company failed to inform us at the time we engaged their services, they require a certified check or cash on delivery. Mrs. Loomis called her bank manager (after hours), and he cashed our check.

Mrs. Loomis suggested that we rent the vacant house previously occupied by one of their maids when she learned of our difficulty finding an apartment. Though wealthy, Dr. and Mrs. Loomis had a common touch. Dr. Loomis washed dishes in spite of having maids. Mrs. Loomis volunteered as an ambulance driver. She re-papered the bathroom in the house we rented from them.

The house we rented presented its own challenges. The first morning after moving in, I went to the basement and found water up to the first tread of the stairs. I called Mrs. Loomis, and she got the local fire station to pump out the water. They cautioned, however, that the water would return unless I installed a sump pump. I followed their advice, solved the problem of water in the basement but created a new one. The length of hose I bought emptied the water onto the driveway, which froze creating a permanent ice rink. Since I had no funds to purchase a longer piece of hose, I skated from my car to my back door every day. Early spring, standing in the yard, a neighbor came to the fence. He introduced himself and told me he wondered why I had the water problem since the house has a sump pump. He told me families in the cul-de-sac where we lived had gotten together and installed sump pumps. Checking afterward, I found a switch tucked under a beam that controlled a sump pump. I wondered why the neighbor waited until the Spring to tell me a sump pump existed when I suffered through the winter. I concluded he probably hesitated to avoid seeming intrusive in my affairs. Did difference in our race have anything to do with his reluctance to approach me sooner? Who knows?

Dane, a first grader, and his younger white friend who lived across the street had been playing in our yard when Dane ran into the house and grabbed a sheet of paper. Soon after, I heard his friend crying. I ran outside to investigate and saw his friend headed for home. I inquired what had happened. Dane told me he and his friend argued about color. His friend described his color as white. Dane called him cream and brought the white sheet of paper to demonstrate the dissimilarity between his color and a white sheet of paper. His friend returned minutes later and said he checked with his mother and she told him he is white. The boys continue as playmates, but I never heard them discuss color again. Denise and the boy's sister became friends and continued to correspond with each other after we moved from Natick.

An incident occurred that demonstrated the gap that existed between blacks and whites in a liberal state as Massachusetts in 1968. Irma and I took friends visiting from New York to a public pond. Arriving, we found many white adults and children enjoying themselves wading throughout the pond. As we entered the pond, all the whites moved to its periphery. The scene soon became a mass of blacks surrounded by a ring of whites. I thought what transpired illustrated how the unfamiliarity between the races breathed distrust.

Living in Massachusetts became stressful for the family. Irma received her nursing license in New York but could not practice in Massachusetts. At that time, individual states issued their licenses. She lived in New York and the rest of the family in Massachusetts. Every Friday, my brother-in-law drove her home to spend time with the family, returning to New York on Sunday in time for work on Monday. Besides the tiring commute and the stress on the entire family caused by the separation, the costs of maintaining the vehicle and two residences became prohibitive. I therefore sought and got an opportunity to continue my studies in New York at Columbia University.

I accepted a position in Buffalo, NY and the family moved to Williamsville, NY a predominantly white community. Sonja our third child and younger daughter attended middle school. In the seventh grade, she excelled in French and planned to continue her studies on the subject in the eighth grade. In spite of her ninety-five percent average at the end of the term, her teacher sent my wife and me a letter stating that she declined to recommend that Sonja continues taking French in the eighth grade. Incensed, I met with the principal the next day and assured him that I would seek reversal of the teacher's decision in whatever forum necessary. I refused to let a white, biased teacher impede my daughter's education. The following day I received a letter from Sonja's teacher stating that she had erred, and Sonja would advance to the eighth-grade French class. I previously heard that white teachers discouraged black students from pursuing academic careers, but refused to think that a teacher could be so blatant in her discrimination. The incident reinforced my belief that black children are disadvantaged without advocacy.

I discovered the difficult challenge faced by students who advance through the education system without acquiring essential knowledge. In 1984, I moved to Washington, DC to establish a healthcare facility. While there, I became a partner in a company that managed a large housing complex in Baltimore, Maryland. In that capacity, I had to confront a tenant whose grandson vandalized one of the laundry rooms. The grandmother could ill-afford to pay for the damage, struggling to take care of her grandson, with one of his parents incarcerated and the other a drug addict, I offered to waive the payment for the damage if her grandson came to see me. I wanted to find out his progress in school. She persuaded him to come to see me by threatening to discontinue his participation in football.

I requested that the grandson, an eighth grader, select a book and bring it with him when he returned to see me in two days. He brought a second-grade level book. He sat in front of me and read in a slow and disjointed manner. His reading incomprehensible, I had him read as I look at the text. As he read, he substituted any word for the ones unfamiliar to him. Now I understood the reason for my lack of comprehension of his previous reading. As a proud person, he tried to hide his poor reading. I tried, without success, to improve his reading and that of some of his classmates. Overcoming the gap between their grade levels and reading comprehension proved insurmountable, due to their level of frustration. The experience prompted me to establish a non-profit organization Saving Our Undereducated and Disadvantaged Black Youth Through Education (S.O.U.N.D.B.Y.T.E.), to help students two or more grades behind at the fourth-grade level. The organization exposed the students to various disciplines by allowing them to interact with chemists, biologists, artists, botanists, etc. at a local university and zoo. I reasoned that enthusiasm for any subject would make the students more attentive to academics in general. The venture showed promise, but the lack of funding caused its discontinuance.

. In high school, my daughter Sonja had an unfortunate experience. The white students refused to let her sit while riding the school bus. They ganged up on her and pushed her off the seats or placed their book bags on the seats to prevent her from sitting. The situation had continued for a week before Sonja brought it to my attention. I refused to get into a protracted argument with the school administration or the white parents and instructed Sonja how to deal with the situation. I told her to knock the book bags off the seat with one hand and swat the student nearest her with the other. Sonja carried out my instruction and reported to me how things went. She told me her actions surprised the white students and the girl she struck froze for a moment then cried as the other girls laughed at her. From that day, Sonja never had a problem getting a seat on the school bus. In fact, many of the girls who previously harassed her became friends.

Another example of poor race relations occurred on a road trip to Buffalo, New York to see my first newborn granddaughter. A highway trooper stopped me. As he peered into the car, he asked, "What do you do?" I ignored his question but gave him my driver's license and registration. He saw a black man in a moderately priced car and decided to challenge me; his stopping me had nothing to do with speeding because I had been driving well within the speed limit.

Nevertheless, he cited me for speeding. I wrote the court disputing the ticket and mentioned the officer's question about what I did. The court, in recognition of the officer's inappropriate behavior, reduced the $250.00 dollar fine to an administrative fee of $30.00.

In race relations, as in other facets of life, actions might be misinterpreted. A couple of incidents illustrate this fact. My wife Irma, other friends and I went to a resort in Catskills, New York for a week's vacation beginning the Friday before Mother's Day weekend. As our cars turned into the driveway headed toward the main building that housed the registration office, we saw several young whites congregated outside. Suddenly, everyone began running and soon disappeared. Perplexed by the reaction, we questioned our "welcome" but decided to overlook it. As we approached the registration desk, the staff's ebullient reception confused us. They inquired about our trip and discussed the week's activities. Later, we asked the resort staff why everyone ran as we approached the registration building. They explained that everyone had to report to his station; we had been the first guests of the season.

After my friend Joel had left to return to New York, the weekend he assisted me to find an apartment before starting classes at Brandeis University, a young white female teacher who had recently moved to the area and stayed at the bed and breakfast as Joel and me, invited me to have dinner with her at a nearby restaurant. We entered the restaurant, sat and waited for a server. Twenty minutes later and no one offered to serve us; we assumed discrimination as the reason. As the thought went through our minds, a white woman who sat several tables from us came over and explained that it was self-service. That experience taught me never to assume anything without investigation.

A couple of race-related experiences occurred in my Brooklyn, New York neighborhood in 1965. Vendors denied a black liquor store owner in my neighborhood certain products. I went to the liquor store to stock up for the Christmas holidays, doubly pleased to patronize the store because of its black owner and it existed in my neighborhood. I ordered quarts of whiskey, but the owner said he only carried the smaller sizes. Disappointed, I wanted to know the reason. He told me the vendors only sold him the smaller bottles of liquor because they made a greater profit on them. To the contrary, he would make a greater profit on the larger volume bottles. The owner's plight reminded of a story I read about Joe Louis, the heavyweight champion. His failed business ventures included a resort. Vendors refused to deliver liquor to his resort in spite of his ability to pay. Another famous entertainer Peg Leg Bates told me he had similar difficulties with vendors when I visited his resort in Kerhonkson, N.Y. while attending a conference.

Oil companies denied credit to a black owner of a gasoline station in my neighborhood, in spite of his credit worthiness. I drove to the gasoline station a couple of blocks from my home. It had streamers and signs hung declaring new ownership. Proud to support a black neighborhood business, I pulled up to a pump. A black attendant came and asked what type of gasoline I wanted. I ordered high-test. He only had regular gasoline. Disappointed, I asked to speak to the owner. He pointed to himself; I told him my elation to patronize a gasoline station owned by a black man, but I felt disappointed the station had no high-test gasoline. The owner went on to tell me that oil companies sell him gasoline on a cash basis. They refused him an account even though he had excellent credit. I started to ask what about a bank but realized how ridiculous my question would be. I knew from personal experience the difficulty blacks have to get credit.

As a credit union member, I sought a loan to replace our car (totaled in an accident), so my wife Irma could come home to Massachusetts on the weekends. The loan officer asked what collateral I had. I told him graduation from my doctoral program. He still insisted I had no right to expect a loan without collateral. With that, I jumped out my chair and shouted, "Here I am a doctoral student, asking to get a loan to buy a car to ensure my future and you refuse to help me." He became very upset, embarrassed by the many faces that peered into his cubicle. The predominantly black and West Indian credit union had many people in office that day. The ruckus that I caused got me the loan. Several years after I had graduated I met the loan officer at a West Indian party. I introduced myself and thanked him for helping to ensure my future.

Chapter Nine
Summers in New York while at College

My first summer in America in 1958 Owen, Keith and I went to New York to socialize with friends and find employment. Owen and Keith stayed at the Beckles on 143rd street in Manhattan -a family they knew from Guyana. Aunt Olive, my parents' friend who lived in Harlem, got me a room in a house on 117th street in Harlem. I slept in my room but spent most of my time with Keith and Owen at the Beckles. The first evening after moving into the room, I returned home from the Beckles and had a surprise. Someone moved inside my room when I opened the door. I closed the door and retreated into the hallway. The elderly woman who lived in the adjacent room heard my footsteps and came out to check. She had heard my door open and close in rapid succession. She asked if I had a problem. I shook my head indicating no but asked if my room had a back door. She looked puzzled by my question but told me no. She went back to her room, and I had to decide whether to enter my room or go back to the Beckles. How would I explain being afraid to enter my room? Pride overcame fear, and I decided to enter my room. I would use an old western tactic learned from movies. I lunged into the room to present a moving target to anyone in there. I expected an attack, but nothing happened. I landed hard on my shoulder and as I raised my head, I saw my reflection in the full-length mirror in the wardrobe facing the door. I had forgotten about the mirror. My reflection had scarred me. Now my shoulder ached terribly, but I consoled myself that I avoided the embarrassment of telling the Beckles I am afraid to enter my room.

I applaud the generosity of the Beckles family. The first two nights in New York, I visited with Owen and Keith I knew no one else in the city. Both nights, the Beckles insisted that I have dinner with the family. The third night I told them I had to leave before dinner because I had to meet someone. They questioned whom I knew in the City since I just came. They encouraged me to stay for dinner, but I declined. I fabricated the appointment to avoid imposing on their generosity.

I have fond memories of the Beckles household. I made a condiments shelf for Mrs. Beckles (Aunt Inez). Dr. Beckles (Uncle Winslow) recognizing that I had some woodworking skill soon found lots of odds and end jobs around the house for me. Friday night Uncle Winslow and the boys gathered around the television to watch the Friday night fights. I loved to talk with Aunt Inez, but I disliked her conversations when she sat beside me as I tried to get into the fights with the fellows. Aunt Inez told many stories. I recall one of them because I thought it funny. It went like this: Uncle Winslow and Aunt Inez while in bed heard a noise on the lower floor of their home. Uncle Winslow went downstairs to investigate. As he stepped onto the lower floor, he confronted a burglar. He and the burglar, surprised to see each other, ran in opposite directions around the stairwell coming face to face once more. They took off in opposite directions again with the same result. After their third face-to-face encounter, Uncle Winslow said to the burglar, "You stupid man, there is the window" - pointing to the window through which the burglar entered the house. The burglar took Uncle Winslow's advice and climbed through the window.

Owen, Keith and I looked for work together. The first time we went out Keith held the money for the subway fare. We took the subway to a certain point and walked from there to various places to look for work. Returning home on the subway after walking many miles in search of work, I sat down while Keith and Owen stood. I realize they had gotten off the train after it left the station. They worried about me because of my inexperience with the subway – a first-time rider. I remained calm and got ready for the adventure. At the next station, I got off and told the cashier in the booth I needed to talk to him without jeopardizing my ability to get back on the train. He gestured for me to approach the booth. I explained what had happened, that I had no money and need to get to 116th street and Lenox Avenue. The cashier gave me a token, pointed out the train to take, and I found my way home.

On a Friday evening, I went to the Beckles' home to meet Owen and Keith. We planned to meet with friends for a night out. They had already gone but left a message for me to meet a female friend of theirs at a bus stop, and wait for them at her home. They would pick me up by 9:00 p.m. I waited until 11:00 p.m. but no one came. Their friend became ill at ease about the late hour and yawned to give me a hint. I bade her good night and left. However, I had a problem – no money to get home one hundred blocks away. I had spent my last dime (the metro fare) to meet the friend. I stood on a busy street in lower Manhattan, a short distance from the friend's home and decided to ask a passerby for a dime to get home. I approached several men and asked for a dime, but they ignored me. I realized I stood close to a bar, which might have given the impression I needed the money for a drink. I moved up the block and after several rejections of my plea, a man stopped and gave me a quarter. I insisted that I only needed a dime; he told me I had better hold on to the quarter in case I lose a dime – very funny!

Keith, Owen and I had friends who epitomized New York – the Adams brothers. They lived there from childhood. We spent many Saturdays with them in Greenwich Village where they introduced me to jazz music, unintelligible to me at the time. I got an up-close look at the drug scene. Hanging out at clubs, strangers invited us to parties. Upon entering, the atmosphere seemed like a foggy night due to the heavy marijuana and cigarette smoke. I avoided marijuana, preferring booze (alcohol). Owen, Keith and I stuck to booze, the amount limited by our meager funds and our conclusion that our lives as black men had enough hardships with all our faculties. We also saw the harmful effects of marijuana and other drugs on individuals around us; particularly young women strung out on heroin.

A female friend invited me to see a play, and we attended a party after to meet the actors and discuss the play. When we arrived at the apartment, the young woman who opened the door sprayed a deodorizer up and down the stairwell. As we entered, I realized she sprayed to counteract the heavy marijuana smoke seeping out. As the evening progressed, a young black man came around with a tray of rolled cigarettes and offered them to the guests – a mixture of blacks and whites. The man next to me and I declined the cigarettes. Our refusal offended the man sharing the rolled cigarettes, and he told us to get off our high horses. His statement pissed me off, and I told him as black men we could ill-afford to addle our brains with drugs. Then, I pointed to the white man asleep under a table and suggested that he offered him my share of the cigarettes. That man, I said, would always have opportunities irrespective of his mental state. The incident reminded me of the time I took "no-doze" tablets, offered me by a student in our group returning a Sunday from an out of town trip. I had to complete a paper for a class at eight the following morning. I took the no-doze tablets in the late afternoon. By eleven at night, I felt sleepy but my paper remained unfinished. Never a coffee drinker, I drank two cups without cream or sugar. I finished my paper but stayed awake the following two nights, unable to sleep. I thought if no-doze tablets (caffeine) had such a drastic effect on me, why I would want to use other drugs. I decided to leave the party but offered the young woman with me the option to remain or leave with me. She left with me.

Chapter Ten
Jobs while in College

I started college 1958 in the middle of the school year, with the hope that I would earn enough money while at school and during the summers to defray my college expenses. A fallacious assumption I discovered because summer jobs paid so little, but I found the experiences priceless.

I worked for seventy-five cents an hour at a restaurant in Springfield Ohio, a town a few miles from the college, cleaning toilets, emptying garbage, sweeping and mopping floors. Although scheduled to work four hours, I usually worked more hour for the same pay because the owner insisted I completed a portion of my job after the patrons left, although I could complete my chores with them present. At night, as I emptied the garbage pails, I extended one leg and an arm holding a pail to open the batwing doors to the dumpster, when the bottom of the pail fell out, and gravy oozed down my pants leg and into my shoes. The discomfort disgusted me, but I muse that a cat would lick me to death if it were to pass by. The light-hearted nature of that thought comforted me, and I finished my chores.

In Manhattan New York, I had a job working with a silk screen. I accepted the summer job with the understanding that I would start at a dollar an hour with an opportunity for an increase of fifty cents depending on my speed. Knowing that I needed to make as much money as possible before I returned to college in a few weeks, I worked very hard to become the fastest among the new hires. I accomplished the task, but when I asked for the wage increase, the owner demurred. I responded by slowing my pace, which resulted in a visit from the shop steward who warned me to maintain my pace or face termination. I knew they liked my work and wanted to keep me; therefore, I ignored his warning. However, in order to ensure I maintained my pace on the assembly line they had me work ahead of the fastest worker in the shop. We printed patterns on placemats, bibs, and similar items. Each pattern had multiple colors applied in succession; each operator's screen added a different color to complete the pattern. Following the discussion about my wage increase, we worked on a placemat with a pattern "Mary had a little lamb" which included Mary, her lamb, and cockleshells. My screen added the first color to the pattern, and I passed it on to the next screen operator (the fastest worker) who added the second color and successive colors added in like manner along the assembly line - twelve colors to complete the pattern. At the end of the run, which comprised of one hundred and forty-four dozen mats, the quality assurance person realized that Mary had no eyes. Pandemonium struck because it meant that someone had to paint in Mary's eyes by hand on every piece. Everyone who worked on the pattern had to clean his screen to determine which screen should have printed Mary's eyes. My screen had the eyes, which had clogged on my screen after a few pieces. Hurried by the fast worker after me, I did not realize the eyes had stopped printing. The owner fussed at me, and I decided to leave the job with the satisfaction that in trying to get me to continue my fast pace, someone had to paint in the eyes by hand.

    A summer in Brooklyn New York I worked two jobs. I worked the evening shift at a hospital and the night shift at a nursing home. When I got to the nursing home, I ate my dinner with a cold soda bought from one of the residents. One night I arrived at the nursing home, but the resident could no longer sell sodas. The administration found out that the resident cooled the sodas in the freezer in the morgue among the corpses.

    One night on my way to the nursing home, I had a foreboding that things would go wrong. My intuition turned out to be correct. An employee left early because of a family emergency, and I filled in for him on the unfamiliar ward. The other orderly on the ward warned me that a bed-ridden resident in my section would ask me to turn him frequently. He suggested that I leave the resident's draw sheet (a small sheet that can be changed without removing all the bedding) untucked to facilitate turning him. A half hour into my shift, a resident called out, "orderly turn me" I went over to the resident's bed and turned him although he seemed to be asleep. Five minutes later, the same voice called out. I went over and turned the resident. Within a few minutes, I had turned the resident twelve times. The last time I went to the resident's bedside, I found him asleep and suggested that he had called me in his sleep. He looked puzzled by my accusation. About to turn the resident once more, I heard the same resident voice call out, and I realize the resident two beds over had been calling and I had been turning the wrong resident. The orderly who warned me pointed in the direction of the resident's bed and told me he had a beard. Unfamiliar with the residents on the ward, I did not realize that several residents had beards. In addition, the resident that needed my attention never called out before, while I stood at the wrong resident's bed.

The night's disaster continued. A resident, over six feet tall weighing two hundred and fifty pounds or more, asked to go to the bathroom but informed me of his inability to walk. Since I weighed one hundred and forty-nine pounds, I decided to offer him a bedpan. He protested using a bedpan and pleaded that I take him to the bathroom. I made a grave mistake by acquiescing to his pleads. I used my training with the disabled to get him into his wheelchair and off to the bathroom. I swung him onto the commode, gave him a roll of toilet tissue and told him to call me when finished. I returned to the resident and found him in feces all over his hands, thighs, and stomach. I had made a blunder. I forgot that without the use of his legs he would be incapable of lifting off the commode to clean himself. To take care of the mess, I dampened a large sheet, lathered it with soap and washed him. Then I needed to get him back to bed. As I lifted him off the commode, his much heavier weight than mine caused both of us to crash to the floor. I called my co-worker to help; he refused to assist, claiming that he had a painful back due to an injury and reminded me that he cautioned me about taking the resident to the bathroom. I struggled for almost an hour to get the resident back to bed.

The drama of the night had just begun. Two residents stood on their adjacent beds pissing at each other. I tried to stop them but became the target. At that moment, I reached my limit of tolerance. I called my wife Irma and asked her to call the nursing supervisor's office and inform them of a family emergency that required my attention. An hour after I had spoken to Irma, no call came from the nursing office. I called the nursing supervisor and accused her of ignoring my wife's call about an emergency at home. The supervisor pleaded for me to stay until the end of the shift; I declined and headed out the door. That ended my summer employment for the year.

At another job in Brooklyn New York, Owen, Keith and I worked as shipping clerks. We selected and set aside boxes of goods for shipment by truck. The building reeked of dust, which required sturdy clothing that could withstand the harsh environment. I wore pants without loops that had lost the waist button, necessitating a belt under my waist to hold it up. One knee of my pants had a large rip, and the sole of one shoe hung loose. I taped the shoe to prevent it hanging and tripping me, but wetting the floor to keep the dust down loosened the tape. Owen and Keith looked at me and suggested that my Mom would cry if she saw me in that condition. They looked just as awful. Moving around the warehouse, I looked an awful sight. I had my left hand above my head holding boxes in place on the hand truck as I pushed it with my right hand, while flipping my right leg as I go along to prevent my loose shoe sole from tripping me.

On an afternoon returning from the shipping clerk job, Owen, Keith and I had an unusual experience. Walking through a vacant lot, a lower window of one of the buildings opened and a large bag filled with garbage came hurtling through the air. Keith caught it and hurled it back into the apartment. We stood for a moment until we heard the bag land with a loud thud and confusion break out. We heard shouting and cursing as we took off. We peeked at the vacant lot a few minutes later and saw several individuals discussing and arguing who could have done such a deed. Continuing on home, we hoped Keith's action deterred future dumping by the family.

I worked in a sweatshop (literally) in Brooklyn, New York. The first day I walked in the shop no one wore a shirt. The workers signaled to me to take my shirt off. I ignored them at first, but the suffocating heat in spite of fans made me toss it within an hour. The shop made aquariums, and I worked with a partner. He assembled the tanks, and I cleaned them. The first day at work, one of my coworkers cleaned some of my tanks. I presumed he helped me out as a new worker. At the end of the day, the supervisor reviewed my performance, and I came up short. My partner had a quota of one hundred small tanks. He made eighty tanks, and I cleaned only sixty of them. My coworker, whom I thought helped me, had helped himself. He received a bonus for every tank he cleaned beyond his quota. For three weeks, I labored at the job keeping up with my partner and occasionally cleaning a few extra tanks from other workers' pile. I had learned the tricks of the job. My job came to an abrupt end when loose glass on one of the tanks ripped my fingers – I used them in a rubbing motion to clean. I had no regrets for the forced resignation because I returned to college a week later.

Chapter Eleven
Musical Exploits

Our college mate John, our bandleader and an ordained minister, played the guitar very well and delivered excellent sermons. He could command the attention of a holy rolling congregation or a reserved one. In Guyana, many knew him for his high-energy sermons. He had spillover attendance at the church where he preached. He came from a religious family. His evangelist parents sang and played the guitar. His older brother (Samuel) ministered as well.

John, a mathematics, and political science major, relished singing and playing the guitar. We jammed in our dorm room. John sang lead, played his little guitar and Owen, Keith, Elwood and I provided background vocals. Elwood drummed on an overturned trashcan, and I shook two boxes of Rice Krispies as maracas. Owen and I entertained our group with an eighteen-inch limbo. Spring and fall students gathered on the lawn outside Owen and Keith's room in the basement of the dorm to listen to us.

Dr. Terry, head of the music department, called John and told him she received an inquiry about students who played Calypso music. A couple wanted a group to play for a calypso party at their country club as a treat for their friends. John phoned and arranged a meeting at the couple's home in an exclusive suburb of Cincinnati.

The couple welcomed us and told us they planned to decorate the main hall of the country club to create a Caribbean atmosphere. They ordered banana trees from Florida, built a bamboo tent with signs notating rumba, cha-cha, meringue, etc. made of the same material.

They bought us a conga drum, amplified guitar, ruffle-sleeved shirts and black three-quarter length pants. They also gave us a pair of maracas, a small bongo drum and a square instrument called a jungle guitar – an instrument unknown to us. We called our group "The Calypso Islanders."

The affair came off as a smashing success. Guests enjoyed doing the limbo, although most of them could only bend back their head. The animated bartender caught up in the spirit of the party told us he worked at the club for ten years and never saw guests and club members enjoy themselves so much. Guests raved about the party, sending the hosts many flattering compliments. The hosts impressed by our performance asked us to play at the club's ball in the fall of the year. That idea overshadowed our success by creating a rivalry between our group and the orchestra that played for the function in the past. The orchestra's leader offered to have our group play during intermissions – an idea acceptable to us, but the ball's organizers rejected the suggestion.

Later that summer, the couple promoted "The Calypso Islanders." They negotiated a contract for us to play at the Wright Patterson Air Base officers' club for the summer. We started at the end of the semester. Owen learned to play the jungle guitar, Keith the bongo drum, Elwood the conga drum. John, the leader of the band, played guitar and sang lead; I played maracas and with Owen performed an eighteen- inch limbo. The lyrics of the Guyana folk songs we sang came from our collective memories. When memories failed, we used West Indian curse words and slang as lyrics. They worked like a charm so much so that at the end of sessions, officers complimented us stating they loved all our songs especially the ones in our language. They mistook the curse words and slang for a foreign language.

A friend and his wife accompanied us to the club as a part of our entourage. On our return home, they told us as they sat in the audience an officer's date got excited as Owen, and I danced and proclaimed, "I'd like to do it with those niggers." The officer, embarrassed, hustled his date out the club.

The sergeant (Sarge) in charge of the officers' mess hall became a fan and hung out with us a lot. Some Saturday nights after our performance, he arranged a sumptuous meal for us in a classy setting with a white tablecloth and fine dinnerware. We enjoyed his conviviality and dismissed rumors of him being gay.

While at the officers' club, we rented the furnished upper apartment of a two-story house with three bedrooms, full dining room, two baths and a large kitchen. The owner lived on the lower floor. Our fans came and went all day long. A rainy morning, the owner went upstairs to close the windows because she thought everyone had left. She pushed a bedroom door left ajar to close any open windows. Seeing John and a girl in there, she apologized, pulled the door shut and left. John went downstairs, berated the owner and left with his girlfriend. When Owen, Keith and I returned, the owner invited us to her apartment. Intoxicated, a revolver and bullets in her hands, she repeatedly vowed that she would make a sieve out of John when he returned. She recounted what had occurred; we coaxed her for quite a while, and she calmed down. We had John apologize when he returned the next day, and that calmed the waters.

On an occasion, Sarge dropped us off home a Saturday morning about four, and we urged him to stay over and go directly to work. He accepted our invitation and slept beside Elwood. We got up after Sarge left, but Elwood remained asleep. Lying on his stomach in a deep sleep, we decided to play a prank on him. We raised his pajamas and poured egg white down the seam of his buttocks. Elwood, startled by the wetness, grabbed his buttocks and jumped up looking at the sticky stuff on his hand and exclaimed, "What the hell?" We looked at him wide eyed; mouths opened and in unison shouted, "Sarge got you!" Elwood got out of bed in a rage grumbling, "Where is he? I'm gonna kill that S.O.B." To further incense him we ragged Sarge did his stuff and left in a hurry. Elwood dressed and headed toward the door on his way to the airbase to confront Sarge. We had intercepted him before he got to the door. Now, we had to convince him we played a prank. He accepted our word after we showed him the discarded eggshell with the yolk.

After three weeks at the club, the authorities terminated our playing arrangement due to our non-union status and pressure from the musician union, which threatened to prevent union bands from playing at the club in the future. That placed the club in an untenable position. The union acted on a complaint from the orchestra leader denied the contract to play for the country club's ball. Our sponsors asked prominent musicians, politicians and clergy to intervene on our behalf, but their efforts failed. Our status as foreign students without work permits precluded us joining the musician union. We left the officers' club after one month.

Friends of the couple (our band sponsors) engaged our band for their parties. The hostess of one of the parties requested that Owen and I not dance. She claimed that our erotic movements disturbed her. At the party, John ignored her request and offered to have Owen and I dance for the guests. Her husband unaware of his wife's request and having seen us dance at the country club cheered and encouraged us to dance. The hostess excused herself and left the room while we danced. She complained to our sponsors after the party, but they overlooked John's intransigence because of the husband's enthusiasm and encouragement and the guests' expressed enjoyment.

John arranged other performances for the band. We performed at the Hudson River festival in 1959, summer- a memorable event for me. We rehearsed at a club in the theater district in downtown Manhattan where we met and spoke with Sydney Poitier as he walked by. The same day, we met one of the Mills Brothers at a recording studio. I danced the limbo in pain, at the Hudson River celebration. A bead dropped from the costumes of the previous Haitian dancers stuck in a blister on the side of my great toe. Later that summer, we recorded an album of Guyanese folk songs titled "The Songs of Guyana Jungle" by "The Potaro Pork knockers" – a name given to gold miners in the interior of Guyana. The album included many traditional folk songs and others composed by us. Today, many of the tunes remain popular in Guyana and throughout the Caribbean. That summer John sang in Greenwich Village coffee shops and Owen, Keith and I dropped by some evenings and sang with him.

We performed at Ohio State University International Club celebrations. Owen and I danced the limbo. Owen started from one side of the limbo pole and I the other; we passed each other under the pole. At an event, as we passed under the pole, Owen fell on his back. I jumped up, flounced around him, helped him off the floor, and we started over. At the reception following our performance, many attendees told us that they really enjoyed the part of the limbo dance when Owen acted as though he fell and I had to help him up. We smiled and accepted the compliments – little did they know!

A friend invited us to Cleveland, Ohio to meet a music promoter to help our calypso group to get more exposure. We arrived at his residence two weeks later. We met his friend at the Majestic Hotel where we subsequently stayed at his expense. After checking in, we accompanied him to meet the famous bandleader Bo Diddley playing in town. The promoter introduced us to Bo Diddley and his band members. I got an opportunity to play maracas with the band and remember a little tune they sang when a group of women got up to go to the bathroom. It went as follows: "We know where they're going, and we know what they're gonna do." We discussed possible engagements for our band and returned to the hotel. The promoter promised to return later that morning to take us to meet others in the music business. At 11:00 a.m., the promoter had not returned, and we decided to have breakfast in our suite. I called the front desk to place an order, and the clerk asked for my credit card; we panicked learning no meals came with our suite. We had no money and no food other than a large box of corn flakes. During the day, each of us had a handful of corn flakes and as much water as our stomach would take. Two days later, and the promoter never appeared. Our friends inquired everywhere for him without success. The promoter had reserved the suite for seven days; on the third day, we found out that we had parked in a private lot and owed fifteen dollars.

Out of corn flakes and hungry, we looked for every opportunity to earn enough money to pay the parking bill and buy gasoline to get us back to campus. We looked up the surnames of our college mates who lived in Cleveland in the telephone directory to no avail. We entered an amateur music competition held in the hotel bar room, won the contest but disqualified because the judges considered our band professional. The second place winner, a female vocalist received the hundred-dollar prize, so we were back to square one. As we left the contest, John recognized a sociology professor whom we met when he visited our college. He told us he lived in Cleveland and suggested we look him up when in the area. John approached the professor who recognized and greeted us. He asked if we stayed at the hotel and invited us to dinner at a Chinese restaurant across the street. At the restaurant, the professor sat and chatted for a while, told the waiter to take our order and excused himself to go to a meeting. We embraced him, thanked him for the dinner and he left. After he had left, we wondered if he had arranged payment of the bill; whether he did or not, we decided to gorge ourselves and wash dishes if necessary. The professor had placed payment of the bill to his account.

Midday the following day and fourth day of our stay, we sat on our beds pondering our next meal. A knock on our door and there stood a man with a Jamaican accent. He introduced himself and said he came because he heard of our band and he wanted us to hear some of his compositions. He sang a song, "'old 'em Medina with the rice and crab, 'old 'em." Unbelievable, we thought how ironic he sang about food as we sat hungrily. We brightened up when he invited us to join his club's cricket match later in the day and have dinner at his home afterward. We played cricket for hours in the extended summer daylight. After a couple hours, I complained of a sprained ankle and sat out the game. How foolish could I be playing cricket in the hot sun on an empty stomach? After the game, we went to the Jamaican's home. The table had many empty dishes, and no food. The five of us (John, Owen, Keith, Elwood and I) looked at each other in wonderment. I approached the woman of the house, explained our circumstance and told her that her husband invited us to dinner. She prepared a big pot of "cook-up" rice, and we had a good meal. The fifth day of our stay we reached a friend in Columbus Ohio who wired us enough money to pay the parking bill and buy enough gas to get us back to campus. By that time, we had heard that the promoter died by gunshot after he dropped us off at the hotel.

Chapter Twelve
My First Jobs Following Graduation

I graduated in January 1962 and returned to New York to seek employment urgently. The college gave me a student copy of my transcript rather than an official one since I owed tuition. I used it to seek employment. Two medical institutions hired me with the proviso that I showed my green card to human resources before reporting to work. I never returned because of my student status.

We expected the birth of our first child in March and had no maternity health insurance, although my wife's employer had assured her otherwise. An employment agency had referred me to two voluntary hospitals. When I informed the agency that the job offers required permanent residence, it sent me to a state hospital hoping the job requirements were different. The state application had two resident categories – citizen or non-citizen. As a non-citizen, I qualified for a laboratory assistant position. A technologist position required American citizenship. I completed an application for the laboratory assistant position, and human resources sent me to the clinical laboratory for an interview.

The supervisor hired me for the position; she reasoned that I needed the job and could perform tasks beyond my official job title. She recognized that my salary would be below my capabilities and reported to the employment agency that she offered the job to someone else. I saved one month's salary.

Sitting in the waiting room of the hospital clinic with about fifteen white women while awaiting my medical examination for the job, the women surprised me by how freely they spoke about their sexual proclivities and obstetric issues. Most people that I knew guard their medical issues especially among strangers, which made their frank discussions in my presence as a black male quite unusual. I also observed that one of the women who mentioned that she had just returned from the dentist had dried blood on her lips and chin. I returned to the laboratory after taking my medical examination and mentioned the women's bizarre behavior to one of my co-workers. He responded, "They're crazy!"

The second day on the job, the man autoclaving the glassware continually talked to some invisible person, often laughing and gesticulating. I mentioned the behavior to the same coworker and he retorted, "I told you those people are crazy!" He made his statement so matter-of-factly that I discounted it. Later in the day, the supervisor asked me to go to the ward and draw a patient's blood. As I left the laboratory, she asked if I had a key. Surprised by her question, I asked why I needed a key. Her replied, "Don't you know that they have to keep the crazy patients under lock and key." I became aware then of the type of facility and the words "state hospital" implied a mental institution. We referred to such facilities in Guyana as an asylum or madhouse (colloquial term).

Institution residents performed various tasks in the laboratory, such as autoclaving glassware and pasting blank labels on empty specimen containers, as part of their therapy. A physician ordered a routine urine test for one of the female residents who worked in the laboratory. The results indicated spermatozoa present. Such a result for a female's urine indicates heterosexual intercourse, so this finding caused a furor. The possibility that a female resident had sex while on a therapeutic work assignment created a serious and possibly litigious problem for the administration. The laboratory supervisor held her head and proclaimed about to have a "shit" hemorrhage as she walked back and forth. She reported the incident to the administration, and a psychiatrist came to investigate. The psychiatrist, looking crazed himself, rushed in the laboratory shouting, "Where is the resident?" His demeanor would have disturbed anyone (sane or insane) and must have been terrifying to the resident. He and the laboratory supervisor interrogated the resident. They insisted that she tell them where she went and with whom, simultaneously threatening dire consequences.

The resident, a German, who spoke little English, shook her head violently but said nothing. Witnessing the scenario, the resident's silence suggested denial or lack of understanding. However, the badgering continued until the resident collapsed in exhaustion. A couple of hours later, as the resident lay exhausted, an orderly walked in the laboratory and requested the results of his urine test. The record showed no urine test results for him. He insisted that he placed a lid he found on his urine specimen and left it on the counter. The orderly had used the lid from the patient's urine specimen as it lay on the counter during processing. The laboratory had tested and reported on the orderly's urine, as the resident's urine. Sadly, the resident suffered from needless mental anguish from the harsh, confrontational interrogation.

Two other incidents tainted the mental institution's reputation during my tenure. The submission from a black technologist won an institution fashion contest. Upon receiving racially explicit hate mail to an article with her picture published in a local newspaper, the institution reversed her first place finish in the competition and awarded it to a white contestant. The second incident involved persons leaving their children in the institution's care while they took extended vacations. Adding to the incredulity of the situation, the children had no mental illness.

On a bright sunny summer afternoon, residents dressed in colorful and well-pressed outfits sat on benches or laid out on the manicured lawns of the institution, as I stood on the steps of laboratory building waiting for a taxi. The taxi arrived and as I got in the driver remarked, "Lots of visitors today!" I replied that they were residents. He looked puzzled and asked, "What type of facility is this?" I told him a mental hospital and sat behind him. He adjusted the rearview mirror to keep me in sight, but I maneuvered as far left as possible, making it difficult for him to see me in the rearview mirror. He continued to adjust the rear view mirror in a vain attempt to keep me in his sight, uncomfortable because he thought I might be a resident. I wanted to make funny faces and abrupt movements to heighten his discomfort but resisted the temptation. We stopped at two traffic lights and each time he adjusted his rearview mirror to see me. At the third traffic light, he could contain his anxiety no longer and said, "Please don't be offended. Are you a resident?" He showed great relief when I told him I worked in the laboratory.

    I had three other jobs while employed at the state hospital. Every evening, I performed patients' pre-operative laboratory tests for a hospital in Manhattan, read blood slides at another in Long Island City and sold vacuum cleaners. I had established hours at the laboratories. The vacuum cleaner company canvassed clients and set up appointments for me, which I kept during down time in the laboratories. The sales job had several exasperating aspects. I dreaded walking up several flights with seven boxes to give a demonstration and return to my car without a sale. Rather than face that scenario, I tried very hard to make my sales. I disliked improvising to demonstrate features of the vacuum cleaner to customers without the appropriate furnishings. For example, illustrating the effectiveness of the vacuum cleaner on carpet and upholstery and the customer had neither. Under those circumstances, I discouraged the customer from a demonstration because they received five dollars with or without a purchase. The company offered the five dollars to customers to get us in the door but became upset when we give out the five dollars without a sale. Surprisingly, many customers who had no need for a vacuum cleaner insisted on a demonstration and often made purchases. Some prospective customers said yes to the canvasser with no intention of receiving the salesperson. Once I arrived at a residence and found a sign on the door that read, "Salespersons and Jehovah witnesses ring this bell at their own risk," and ferocious sounding dogs barked as I approached the door. Using my better judgment, I never touched that bell.

Chapter Thirteen
Handling Money

In my early days at college, Irma and I conducted our business without a bank account. We paid all bills in cash, including my tuition. Carrying cash, I exercised great caution when I traveled by car with other students. I thought it prudent to be cautious rather than sorry. The night before a road trip, I sewed my money in a pocket and placed about ten safety pins around it. I made it as difficult as possible for anyone to get to my money should I fall asleep. During a trip back to campus, we had an accident. The driver's girlfriend, sitting in the back seat served cake to everyone. The driver, instead of raising his hand to receive the cake, turned around taking his attention from the road. At that moment, he lost his bearings slammed the car into a guardrail. The impact broke the right front axle and bent the fender into the wheel preventing it from turning. We called a tow truck, which took us twenty miles to a gas station where we slept in the car until it opened later in the morning. The manager of the gas station quoted a prohibitive amount to replace the axle; the owner of the car decided to replace it himself if the manager instructed him where to acquire one from a junk yard and allowed him to work under the shed where the tow truck parked the car. The manager cooperated recognizing that as students we had limited funds. We bought a used axle from a nearby junkyard, and the student owner of the car (an amateur mechanic) replaced the axle.

Everyone had to pitch in to defray towing costs, the cost of the axle and additional gasoline. First, we pitched in for the towing, and then the axle and several times for gasoline as we traveled. Each time I excused myself and went to the bathroom to retrieve money from my pocket. The first time I had to take the pins out and pull the thread. Thereafter, I had to remove the safety pins that I replaced each time I went in my pocket. Recognizing that I went to the bathroom each time I needed to contribute, the boys ragged that I got diarrhea each time I had to pay up. The story spread when we returned to campus, and I had to put up with the teasing for quite a while.

Chapter Fourteen
Family

I got married December 1959, the same month my father died. He had sent his blessing for my marriage. My Dad adored my fiancée and expressed great joy that our wedding would take place the day after Christmas, as his and Mom. The Adams brothers' mother agreed to have the reception at her home. Shortly after receiving word about the wedding, my Dad met a woman at the bank where he worked. Recognizing she lived in New York, he mentioned my upcoming wedding there. The woman told him that she had recently received a letter from her sons asking permission for their friend to have his wedding reception at their home. She asked my Dad for my name and discovered they referred to the same wedding. He had met Mrs. Adams.

Unable to travel to my father's funeral in Guyana saddened me. Mom dismissed any notion of me going to the funeral. She insisted that Dad would have thought me foolish to jeopardize my future by spending my limited funds to see him dead. What she said made sense with my college fees in arrears and my struggle to bring them current.

The New Year's Eve after Dad's death, I celebrated his life. My father celebrated that night each year with gaiety. He and Mom had attended midnight service before he went off partying with friends. Mom disliked the party scene preferring to stay at home with us children. Dad returned home New Year's morning, and as he entered our street, he wished the neighbors a "Happy New Year" before coming home.

Irma and I attended a New Year's party, and I danced a lot in honor of my Dad. Folks at the party expected us to be sad and mournful over Dad's death. However, they understood when we explained our way of celebrating his memory. On our way home, Irma and her friend Olive removed their shoes and walked barefooted to avoid the pain inflicted by the cheap shoes they bought on sale – a great bargain they thought. Without a car, we had to walk to the subway. On our way, a stranger offered us a ride home. To my surprise, Irma and Olive usually distrustful of strangers accepted the ride. I guess their aching feet motivated them. We got home safely.

My friend, who should have met me on my arrival in America, offered to be best man at our wedding. A few days prior to the date, he called to find out what time to expect the limousine. We informed him that our budget precluded such expenditure. We never heard from him again.

My cousin's husband, a minister, offered to conduct the marriage ceremony at his church in Manhattan. The bride and maid of honor dressed at their residence above the church. As Owen, Keith, Wilmot (another friend) and I prepared to leave home in Brooklyn to take the subway to the church; someone knocked on our door. A friend Samuel, John's brother – also a minister, dropped by. Keith excited to see him blurted out, "Sammy, great to see you! Eric is getting married today, and you're on time to take us to the church." Getting over his surprise, Sammy told us that he would have loved to stay for the wedding but had to finalize his sermon for the next day's service. He also questioned how we had planned to get to the church without his car. Keith responded, "Come on Sammy, you are a man of the cloth. You know the Lord does not come, but he sends." Sammy smiled and agreed to drive us to the church. The wedding went well. Ivan, a friend, snapped pictures. Sammy drove the bride, groom, maid of honor and Aunt Inez (who brought the rice) to the reception. Everyone else had to hit the subway to the reception. Meigan and other friends cooked food for the reception, with little expense to Irma and me. Relatives sent liquor from Guyana for the occasion, and everyone had a rollicking good time celebrating our marriage and the yuletide.

After marriage, we continued to live in a furnished efficiency on Marcy Avenue, in Brooklyn, New York Friends Berry and Elaine (newlyweds as well) and another friend, John, moved into two efficiencies on the lower floor of the townhouse. We supported each other. Irma and I owned a single piece of furniture - a sofa bed that we bought for its utility, instead of a regular chair. It helped to accommodate our friends, mostly fellow students, who came to visit on weekends during the summer to eat cook-up rice – a popular West Indian dish.

We had a houseful of friends on our first anniversary. The efficiency had limited seating, so the majority of our friends sat on the bed. We had lots of fun until the party came to an abrupt end when the bed crashed from excess weight. I used clothes hangers to put it together after everyone left. We lived in the efficiency until shortly before the birth of our first child, Denise. We needed bedrooms but had difficulty renting an apartment. At the time, owners refused to rent to families with children. No housing discrimination laws existed. Irma had to disguise her pregnancy, when we applied to rent an apartment on Jefferson Avenue, in Brooklyn.

The day of Denise's birth, I hurried to the hospital stopping on the way to buy a dollar's worth of flowers for Irma. Happy to see mother and baby doing well when I arrived at the hospital, my spirits dampened when presented with the hospital bill. We had no obstetric insurance and owed the hospital six hundred dollars. A hospital employee had told Irma before I arrived that unless we paid the bill, she could leave the hospital, but the baby had to stay at a cost of thirty-five dollars a day. We never verified the accuracy of the warning. Things worked out in the end when a good friend lent us the money to pay the bill.

I received my paycheck the day Irma and Denise came home from the hospital. Without a bank account, I had to get to a check-cashing store to purchase food for the family. Irma recalls standing at a window as I passed the apartment with lots of snow on my head. The owner of the check-cashing store had just locked his security gate when I arrived. I grabbed his lapels, steered at him and shouted, "You have to cash my check. My baby needs food!" The store owner stood bewildered as I repeated myself. He said nothing but opened the store and cashed my check. I thanked him immensely and headed to a grocery. We opened an account at a credit union with my next paycheck, so I never went back to the check-cashing store, but I always acknowledged the store owner when I saw him. Two years later, I introduced him to my Mom. He told her that what he did for me, he never did for anyone else. He explained to her that he helped me because he sensed my desperation.

Irma and I experienced difficulty taking care of our newborn as two working parents. A friend's mother offered to babysit Denise during the day. A great help but we struggled going back and forth to the babysitter and work using public transportation. I had a great adventure traveling on the bus with Denise as an infant in my arms and the bag with her formula and other supplies on my shoulder. Curiously, women offered their seat, but men never did.

Two months on my job, I bought a 1954 Mercury car for seventy-five dollars. It enabled me to work four jobs simultaneously and take Denise to and from the babysitter. Late picking up Denise a night, Irma went to get her. Without a means to let Irma know I am on the way to the babysitter (no one had cell phones at the time), I arrived a few minutes after she had left with Denise in a taxi. I caught up with the taxi and signaled the driver to stop. Looking scared, he locked the taxi doors and waved me off, but opened them upon Irma's assurance. Later, the taxi driver explained he thought my wife had escaped from the home with the baby after a family dispute.

My mother-in-law urged us to send Denise to Guyana to relieve us of her care as we stabilized our financial situation and I continue my studies. I declined her offer because the family as a unit needed to face its challenges. My Mom came from Guyana to live with us after the birth of our son Dane. The children adored her as she doted on them.

Soon after Mom arrived from Guyana, I returned from work one evening and found a note in our mailbox from an immigration officer. It stated that immigration records showed I came to the country as a student, but there is no indication that I left. The note also requested that I call the immigration service at the number indicated on it. I showed the note to Mom and Irma. It unnerved them, and they urged me to call right away. I declined to tell them that someone might be trying to kidnap me, although the note seemed authentic. A month elapsed, and I found a second note from the same immigration officer in our mailbox. Mom and Irma continue to insist that I pay attention to the notes. We contacted an immigration attorney, even though we had to divert funds from other living expenses to do so. The attorney filed a petition for immigration to hold my passport in the docket (a legal term), which meant that immigration would take no action against me and when Irma became a citizen she could file a petition for me to become a permanent resident. In the meantime, the attorney gave me his business card with a name and a floor number handwritten on the back. The information pertained to my attorney's contact at immigration. He told me to carry it at all times and present it to anyone who attempted to arrest me. Many aggressive immigration agents waited until the weekend to apprehend persons in an illegal status because they might have difficulty contacting their attorney. The contact person information safeguarded me against such action by presenting the card to the agent. My immigration status remained in abeyance until Irma became a citizen and I received my permanent resident status. I remained a permanent resident beyond the four years that made me eligible to apply for citizenship. The requirement of citizenship for a government position in New York City prompted me to apply for citizenship. I became a US citizen the day that British Guiana became independent in 1966.

Mom and Irma had a wonderful relationship. Everyone, other than relatives and close friends, mistook Mom for Irma's mother due to their closeness. They really enjoyed each other's company. They loved watching wrestling. I would come home at night and hear them shouting and animated as they watched matches on television. I entered the bedroom one night to an incredible scene. Mom had Irma in a scissor lock as they rolled on a bed giddy over the wrestling match. So wrapped up in the wrestling, they had maneuvered themselves into the position; I switched off the television to calm the excitement. Mom lived and traveled with us everywhere as an integral member of the family, until her death.

Our friends, Desmond and Greta, bought a two family property on Hageman Avenue in Brooklyn, New York and we rented the upper apartment. The move saved us from the deteriorating condition of the apartment where we lived at the time. At that apartment, the defective furnace spewed black soot with small bits of coal, through the vents. We ran our vacuum cleaner continuously to collect the charcoal particles in the air. We called the owner but received no relief. Fearful of the potential damage to our children's lungs, we called the fire department. When they were on their way, I informed the property owner by phone. She arrived a few minutes before the fire department and stood at the front door of our apartment townhouse. As firefighters approached the property with pick axes, the owner, a West-Indian woman, gesticulated frantically while screaming, "Doan breakup me house!" After inspecting our apartment and the furnace, the fire department issued her a written warning to fix the furnace to avoid a fine. She fixed the furnace temporarily, but its malfunction remained a recurring problem, and we had to move.

Desmond and Greta's family and our family had an endearing relationship and shared the same social group. Our children who are of similar age grew up together and have friendships that endure. Our master bedroom opened onto the roof of the two-car garage; Desmond and I enclosed the space with a wire fence and used it for social events. Denise and Dane learned to ride their bicycles up there.

Dane had attacks of croup (a respiratory condition) as a child and we rushed him to the emergency room on several occasions because he had difficulty breathing. The emergency room refused to treat him because of our lack of health insurance. Our friend Dr. King, a family physician, rescued us. The fact that an emergency room in America would deny care to a young child with difficulty breathing vexed and perplexed us. We found relief for Dane, but other parents languished in despair without a solution. Ironically, Dane, the little boy turned away from emergency care, currently takes care of others as a board certified emergency room physician. Emergency rooms could no longer turn away patients, but too many citizens have no access to primary care.

Mom had been active throughout her life; she never lay in bed due to illness. In America, she sometimes shopped on her own and brought the packages to the top of the stairs, in spite of our insistence that she ask for help. She joined a church and went on excursions. Every August she visited relatives and friends in New

Jersey. On Sundays after church, she stopped at Dr. Peters her physician and a family friend to chat or get her periodic medical checkup. Mom monitored her diabetes by testing her urine daily. In summer of 1968, she returned from a vacation to relative and friends. She told Irma and me that the level of sugar in her urine had increased. Dr. Peters ordered a blood glucose test and when the results came back elevated he instructed Irma (a nurse) to give Mom an injection of insulin. Her blood sugar normalized according to the follow-up blood test. My brother-in-law came from Guyana the same day Mom had the issue with her blood sugar, and she made a puzzling statement to him, "Boy, you come in time for the funeral." She seemed fine during the remainder of the day; she even made her scrumptious meat patties that we devoured. Another relative arrived from London in the evening, and we stayed up until 1:00 a.m. before going to bed. Irma and I heard a knock on our bedroom door, and we thought Mom knocked to wake us as she had done in the past to make sure we had not overslept I opened the door, and Mom said, "Son I'm wheezing." We gave her orange juice in case her blood glucose had dropped too much because she was unaccustomed to insulin by injection. She took oral insulin.

Irma and I decided to take her to the hospital three blocks away where she worked. Desmond (who lived on the lower floor) and I took Mom down the stairs in a large chair over her objections. Mom walked from the front door to the car. In the car, she said, "Jesus, Jesus" - her last words. Irma and I thought that once we got her to the hospital, she would be fine. However, in spite the efforts of the house physician at the small hospital, Mom died. Our children had slept through the commotion of getting Mom to the hospital and expressed disbelief when we told them that she had died, upon our return home from the hospital.

Mom died on a weekday and relatives, and close friends got word of her death, either on the way to work or just as they arrived. They turned back and came to our home. A friend, Joycelyn, had her husband Roddy bring clothes for her and stayed with us for two weeks. The outpouring of grief by all who knew Mom demonstrated how much they revered her. Her sudden death had folks in the neighborhood inquiring about her for weeks later because they missed her. It took me an entire year to stop thinking of her in my conscious moments. Mom's death created an unexpected expense, but with the help of the owner of Lane's Funeral Home (in our neighborhood) and wonderful friends, we laid her to rest.

Following Mom's death, we looked for ways to make family life easier. Irma and I asked our landlord's permission to place a washer and dryer in our apartment to eliminate trips to a Laundromat. They declined our request because of possible water overflow causing property damage, a logical concern. Their denial spurred us to consider home ownership, and we explored the possibility. Our bank pre-approved a mortgage, and we contacted a real estate broker – a sole proprietor who operated from his car. The first offer we made the white seller accepted then rejected it because her sister refused to live next door to blacks. In 1968, housing discrimination laws passed but enforcement lagged.

The next house the broker showed us cost more than our approved mortgage. Surprised that he showed us such an expensive property, he explained that he wanted us to see the property to make a comparison with a property in our price range he intends to show us. The house had carpeting throughout, four bedrooms, a finished basement, two full baths and a half bath. The house in our price range he showed us afterwards had no carpet, one full bath and a half bath, four bedrooms and a finished basement with a commercial style bar with a highly polished counter, a brass foot rail, a beer tap that connected to beer kegs, a sink, twelve bar stools and a functional cash register. In addition, it had flashing and rotating lights surrounding advertisements for various brands of beers and liquors. The seller told us the previous owner operated a commercial bar in the basement. The broker recommended improvements to make the current house comparable to the previous house we had seen. His recommendations made sense. We purchased the property. As recommended, within a year we added a half bath in the large cedar closet on the upper floor, a shower to the basement bathroom, and installed carpeting.

Some of my friends referred to me as "Brother Clarke". They adopted the name from Irma's beloved cousin (Cuz) who came from Guyana to help with the children. She called me by that name as a form of respect even though my elder. Attending a party, an individual I met asked me the name of my church. Puzzled, I inquired the reason for his question. He told me he overheard others call me Brother Clarke that suggested to him someone affiliated with a church in a high position. My friends, overhearing our conversation, laughed and told him he would think otherwise if he knew me better.

Our family enjoyed the years spent on 234th Street in Queens, New York. In our home, we accommodated my nephew, Irma's sister, and my mother-in-law's friend and her two sons, as well as our family. Living with us, they completed their education and established purposeful lives. We appreciated the relationship with the residents on our block, most of whom were black. Most whites except two families had moved, due to "blockbusting." An elderly white couple lived next door; a white woman and her son in his twenties lived across the street. The black families had children of similar age who enjoyed playing in each other's backyard, which provided a secure environment. We celebrated occasions together such as birthdays, births and anniversaries. Irma and I held many parties; our New Year's Eve parties became a popular event. We had a pious elderly woman (Mother H) who lived across the street from us with her daughter and her family. One afternoon, our German shepherd bounded through the door before I attached the leash and ran to Mother H, as she stood frozen. When I reached Mother H, the dog stood looking up at her. At that point, I asked a silly question and got an unexpected answer. I asked, "Did he scare you?" and she blurted out, "He scared the shit out of me!"

The men on our block formed a neighborhood watch group linked to one in an adjacent community that had communication equipment. We had lots of fun touring the neighborhood and probably missed would-be burglars because of closed eyes due to laughter. We invited the young white man who lived across the street from me to join the neighborhood watch. He declined stating, "I just want to get the hell out of the neighborhood." I never thought him a racist but just "out of place" among older black men.

Chapter Fifteen
Educating Our Children

Our older children, Denise, and Dane attended kindergarten at the community center of a public housing complex directed by a great educator, Mrs. Bernstein. I served as president of the school and wrote children stories for its newsletter. The knowledge our children exhibited after leaving the school amazed their first-grade teachers; especially the way they breezed through their entrance examination. Our younger daughter Sonja enrolled in a highly publicized and expensive kindergarten with less stellar results.

Denise and Dane attended the Concord Baptist church school in Brooklyn. Denise matriculated through the second grade and Dane part of his first grade. While in first grade, Denise accompanied me to my laboratory after school where she observed my work and completed her homework. Traveling from school to the laboratory and home, we sang Nat King Cole songs. Her ability to sing "Mona Lisa" in its entirety amazed many adults. She loved to sing the song "Downtown," popular at the time.

The Concord Baptist School gave the children lots of homework that amazed my mother-in-law, a school principal in Guyana visiting us. She and the children spent three hours each night doing homework. Controversy continues about the value of homework. I believe it reinforces instructions received in school and prepares a student for new information. It also inculcates study habits that endure throughout academic years and beyond.

Denise and Dane went to Brooklyn Technical High School – one of the magnet schools in New York City along with Stuyvesant High

School and Bronx High School of Science. Students passed a special examination to attend them. Our younger daughter, Sonja missed an opportunity to sit for the examination because we moved to upstate New York.

We did not have cable television at home while Dane and Denise attended college. Dane, an avid basketball player, wanted cable television to have access to as many games as possible. He asked his Mom and me to add cable to our television service. We turned down his request. He offered to pay for it. To his surprise, we agreed. As he turned away with a smile, I asked him for his new address. He looked at me quizzically. I told him he would have to leave if he must have cable television; that ended the discussion on the topic. Irma and I thought cable television an unnecessary distraction as the children started college. Dane's success at his studies with minimum effort reminded me of my college mate and very dear friend Keith who, though brilliant with a photographic memory, never finished college. With his photographic mind, he breezed through most subjects. He lacked the patience for subjects that demanded a concentrated effort, although extremely capable of mastering any subject. At college, Keith, Owen and I experienced hardships due to inadequate finances. Owen and I, however, endured them better than Keith did. The school physician gave Keith, as a foreign student, a medical excuse to leave college for a year. Keith intended to use the time to work in New York to raise enough money to return to college financially secured. He did not return to college; his plans never materialized. But, he succeeded at a job he held for many years, raising through the ranks due to his brilliance. Unfortunately, when the organization dismantled he lacked the formal credentials to move on.

I believe children should be exposed to and knowledgeable about as many professions and vocations as possible. My son Dane's experience while in college affirmed my belief. Dane, like most students, had difficulty deciding on a course of study. In his junior year, he leaned toward computer science. At the time, he had just begun to work three hours a day Monday through Friday as a kitchen helper in the dietary department of a local hospital. Two weeks before graduation, he walked into our den and told his Mom and me that he had something important to tell us; he had decided to change his major to biology because he wanted to study medicine. Surprised, we inquired how he could make the change at that late stage. He assured us that he had enough credits. He also asked for and received our full support to begin graduate school while he studied and took the medical aptitude examination.

Upon graduation from college, he began a master's degree program at the Roswell Institute, in Buffalo New York, which he completed while in medical school. Though a brilliant student and a member of the National Honor Society in high school, Dane never showed an interest in the natural sciences. At my urging, he participated in a summer science internship at The Roswell Memorial Institute during his senior year in high school. As a scientist, I tried to engage him in scientific discussions during the internship with limited success. I believe that something in his hospital experience inspired him to study medicine. He enjoyed his three-hour a day job so much that he occasionally refused to stay away from work so he could travel with the rest of the family.

Irma and I established specific rules as a guide for our children in our absence. We implemented them from their early years in elementary school. We insisted that they refuse rides from anyone, including relatives and friends unless we gave them instructions to do so. In spite of our admonishment, our son Dane accepted a ride home with a neighbor who went to meet her children at school. His sister Denise refused the ride and walked home through heavy rain without an umbrella. Dane arrived home before Denise and stood outside in the rain until Denise arrived. I welcomed them as they entered the house and hurried them to change out of their wet clothing. I expressed my sadness that they had left their umbrellas at home. Then, Denise reported that Dane rode home with the neighbor and got wet because he stood outside to wait for her; reluctant to let us know he left her to walk home alone. The revelation of his actions in spite of our instructions got him a good whipping – we never had a recurrence of his behavior.

One afternoon a very good friend Roddy, whom the children address as Uncle Roddy, went to our home. Denise and Dane, the only ones home, looked through the window and greeted him. They waved and spoke to him through the window. Later that evening, Roddy called us to commend the children's behavior. He had stopped by the house to use the bathroom. He never asks to use the bathroom, but from the children's demeanor, he realized quickly that he had to find one elsewhere. Irma and I insisted that the children follow our instructions, but we explained our reasons for the instructions so that they could make reasoned judgments if conditions change without violating the basic tenets of the original instructions.

We had specific rules as our children aged to attend functions on their own, prior to going away to college. They could remain at a party for its duration, and I dropped them off and picked them up. We instructed them to call prior to the end of a function if concerned about unsavory activities; I would go for them. I remained at home when they attended a function to be available. Today, the ubiquitous nature of cell phones provides greater mobility. When I went to pick up the children, I took their friends who lived in our neighborhood home as well.

Support Groups

Our family and others formed a support group that nurtured our children through their formative years into adulthood. We melded into a close-knit unit, spent summer vacations together, rotated the celebration of holidays at our homes, cooked out and played games in the park on weekends, and celebrated birthdays and individual achievements. Parents, as a group, went on vacations to the Catskills, Poconos, and Atlantic City. We attended West-Indian dances at such places as the Audubon Ballroom a favorite haunt and place of Malcolm X's assassination.

.I co-founded a more broad-based support group, The Caribbean United Service Association (CUSA) - Its motto: "Each One Help One". Membership consisted of Americans and persons from the Caribbean. We met once a month at members' homes on a rotating basis, shared information, benefitted from individual member's expertise, supported each other's businesses or professions and helped each other in every possible way.

In our support group, we parents never pressured our children to perform but conveyed our expectations and the children's responsibilities. The children motivated each other throughout the years resulting in their success as physicians, nurses, scientists, educators, engineers, judges and attorneys. As regards to our children, Denise, and Dane (closer in age) challenged each other. For example, in a school assembly Dane (a first grader) when asked what he wants to achieve in class replied, "Never miss a word in spelling like my sister." Sonja received her inspiration to aspire to excellence from her older brother and sister. Our children, as the other children in our cohort of families, did well. Denise is a principal of a high school, Dane a board certified emergency room physician and Sonja a registered nurse.

Through the years, the children from our support group of families have developed a special bond that endures, as they became adults and many of them parents.

Chapter Sixteen
The Impact of Language, Culture and Discipline on the Possibilities for Success

I observed that, in America, a language linked to an ethnic or national identity had a significant impact on the success of a professional service or business. My friend, Dr. D, a dentist, originally from Haiti, had been concerned about his ability to succeed in private practice. Consequently, he acquired a master's degree in public health hoping to get a job in the public sector. After graduation, public service jobs difficult to attain, he decided to start a dental practice in his home. Unexpectedly, his dental practice skyrocketed in popularity. The clamor for his services came from his compatriots, many of whom had the little utility of English. Dr. D explained to me that his patients welcomed the opportunity to communicate in their language. They no longer had to rely on someone, possibly one of their children, to translate their dental needs. Another factor, many of his patients liked the social atmosphere of his office because they could engage each other in discourse since they shared similar backgrounds. They felt relaxed and assured when they visited his office. Additionally, the response from the Haitian community allowed Dr. D to expand his services from general practice to specialties in dentistry.

Businesses succeeded because of their patrons' language constraints and cultural identity, and others failed because those factors are missing. However, the language could be a double-edged sword. The purveyor of services benefits from their clients' deficiency in English, but the client's prospects for advancement in the society diminish unless they overcome their deficiency. Cultural norms transferred to American life are helpful to their adherents, even those without language constraints. For example, Guyanese and immigrants from other Caribbean countries living in America continue to utilize a system for saving called a "su-su," payday club or other names. The system allows participants to contribute to a fund and receive the maximum they eventually contribute before they had made the full contribution. For instance, if fifty-two persons contributed one hundred dollars each week for fifty-two weeks, at the end of that period each person would have contributed fifty-two hundred dollars. Beginning week one, a participant receives fifty-two hundred dollars even though that individual has contributed only one hundred dollars. That participant continues to contribute one hundred dollars for the next fifty-one weeks. Individuals in low-paying jobs had been able to make substantial purchases such as a house, by utilizing the system. By contributing one hundred dollars in a fifty-two-month plan, an individual can amass over twenty thousand dollars in four years – a significant down payment on a house. Many of my relatives and friends achieve home ownership utilizing such a system, even though they might have been low wage earners.

Discipline is crucial to enhancing one's possibilities for success in America. Our children, in the third and fifth grades, had been latchkey kids when we returned to New York from Massachusetts. There has been much controversy about children at home unsupervised; however, our children prospered under those circumstances. We instructed our children when they got home to lock the door, do their homework, do not go outside and do not let anyone in. No one meant "no one." A person's connection to the household makes no difference. The rule stands for everyone unless we give specific instructions otherwise.

Our children attended Rosedale elementary school in Rosedale, New York. Our two older children about to graduate to middle school, I decided to ask the principal to recommend a good private school. Irma and I had decided to send our children to private school to avoid the rowdy and undisciplined environment of the public school. At my meeting with the principal, I explained why I went to see him. After my explanation, he looked at me bemused and began laughing uncontrollably. When he stopped, he said to me, "There are rowdy and undisciplined environments in every school public and private; however, you control how your children function in any environment." He went on to tell me that his children, all of whom are professionals, attended public school through high school. The principal then gave advice on how to prepare my children for school, which I found invaluable throughout my children's schooling. He advised as follows: Dress your children as students. They are going to a learning institution, not a fashion parade; let your daughters wear long pants under their skirts and stay out of the stairwell unless transferring from one class to another; your children should use the restroom only during recess. Using the restroom when the class is in session, they are vulnerable because they are isolated from everyone else.

Epilogue

I wrote the account of my experience in America over fifty years as a foreigner to inform prospective immigrants with backgrounds dissimilar to white America of the opportunity that awaits them and their personal responsibility to contribute to the realization of the country's unfulfilled promise to some of its citizens.

Immigrants must prepare themselves as much as possible prior to their arrival, but preparation and skills are often insufficient to succeed in the country. Discipline is crucial, and they must remember that progress is incremental. A plan is necessary, and adherence to it with periodic modification essential. Be aware there are no short cuts to success. Self-reliance is one of the most important traits to propel an individual's progress, although alliances with other progressives provide important support for your efforts.

There is no room for discouragement. Many aspects of American life would be alien to your customs and upbringing. Assimilation to the Country's myriad facets should be gradual but continual. There are many obstacles to overcome. White society guards its privilege, resisting anyone who dares to wrest any portion of it from them. Any hope of intruding into their sphere of privilege depends on preparation through education and the inculcation of high standards.

Many individuals in American society would attempt to impede your progress; others would lend a helping hand. You must position yourself to take advantage of every opportunity. Never compromise principle in hopes of creating opportunity, because opportunity obtained in that manner is fleeting and undesirable.

Never consider obstacles as problems, because inherent in problems is defeat. Consider them challenges, which respond to determined and continual effort. Adoption of such a strategy by individuals in this society, with its changing demographics, ensures their gradual ascension.

I present my lighthearted and troubling experiences - a reflection of life. In the end, we determine our happiness and others might enhance it.

www.ingramcontent.com/pod-product-compliance
Lightning Source LLC
Chambersburg PA
CBHW071725040426
42446CB00011B/2215